JOHN TOVEY'S
COUNTRY
WEEKENDS

JOHN TOVEY'S
❦COUNTRY❦
WEEKENDS

EBURY PRESS
LONDON

Published by Ebury Press
Division of The National Magazine Company Ltd
Colquhoun House
27–37 Broadwick Street
London W1V 1FR

First impression 1988
Text copyright © 1988 John Tovey
Illustrations copyright
© The National Magazine Company Limited

ISBN 0 85223 616 6

Edited by Veronica Sperling and Susan Fleming
Art direction by Frank Phillips
Photography by Jan Baldwin
Styling by Kathy Sinker
Design by Bill Mason

Filmset by Advanced Filmsetters (Glasgow) Ltd
Printed and bound in Italy by New Interlitho S.p.a., Milan

Cover photograph shows a dinner in the garden at Miller Howe:
Smoked Salmon in Walnut Spinach Nest with Poached Egg and
Hollandaise (page 138); Roast Guinea Fowl (page 139); Syllabub
(page 139); Simple Wine Jelly (page 140) and shortbread fingers.

CONTENTS

Introduction 6

Breakfasts and Brunches 9

Light Lunches, Picnics and Barbecues 32

Afternoon Teas 64

High Teas 84

Suppers 100

Dinners 126

Edible Gifts 146

Index 156

Acknowledgments 160

INTRODUCTION

Let's start off by being completely honest with one another, or else the point of the book will be lost. It is lovely having friends round for dinner or to stay for the weekend – but only as long as everything goes according to plan. You, like me, must have many times said on the day, "Why, oh why, have I lumbered myself with these guests when I've had an awful week at work, my feet ache, my back hurts, and my nerves are tense. I could well do with somebody looking after *me* rather than the boot being on the other foot." If this is the case, you haven't planned well in advance, and are simply not basically 'trained' in the art of entertaining – for believe you me, entertaining is just that . . . an *art* that can be learned.

Having guests for the weekend obviously does mean more washing up, more mess in general (let *them* help, they'll want to anyway if they're any sort of friends), but weekend *cooking* should involve the absolute minimum of work, allowing you as host/hostess the maximum amount of time with your guests to walk, talk, drink, play etc. What *is* required is that little (and I truly mean *little*) extra effort at each meal cooked during the working week, and a sensible utilizing of your fridge, freezer and other storage facilities.

As you glance through the recipes, you'll see more clearly what I mean but, in general, common sense should prevail. If you're making a pastry pie during the week, make *extra* pastry, freeze as a base, and then you have part of a meal ready for the weekend. And when cooking vegetables during the week, prepare a few more than you need immediately; store in the fridge or freezer, and you will have the basis of a vegetable quiche, soup or accompaniment. The same with meats: the leftovers of roasts can be simply sliced and stored in the fridge ready for weekend sandwiches, or transformed in the processor into a meat filling for a pastry case or a pie etc. Only in this way can a canny weekday cook become a contented and charming host/hostess during the weekend.

Most of the recipes in this book are relatively inexpensive – a change for me! – and some are downright 'cowboyish', possibly to be frowned upon by the foodies. But, believe you me, they *work*, and have all been thoroughly enjoyed by my house guests at Brantlea and at Willow Farm in Crawshawbooth (my two homes in, respectively, Bowness on Windermere and the Rossendale Valley in Lancashire). By taking these shortcuts I have had the fun of really enjoying my guests' company: catching up on nice gossip, playing Scrabble, walking with Ossie, my dog, on the fells and moors, sitting sipping pre-lunch gin and tonics on the lawn, then possibly having just that little extra glass of wine at lunch and snoozing it off in the afternoon. After all that, I will feel fit and ready to get cracking with the preparation for the evening meal, joyfully unloading the dishwasher and laying the table (often fitting in some jobs for the next morning's breakfast).

The one thing I would like you to get instilled in your mind *now* is that everything you do when having guests for the weekend should be at *half* the normal pace of during the week. I remember staying with some new-found acquaintances and becoming more and more uptight and tense as the weekend progressed. She was constantly rushing everywhere, shaking and plumping up cushions, taking things hurriedly and noisily out of cupboards, slamming oven doors, speedily removing dirty dishes, frantically washing up and drying at a rate of knots, blowing into the lounge like a March gale with a painfully frozen smile; it all resulted in dishes being broken, food being spoiled, and the whole two days a horrible nightmare.

My solution to the 'problem' is to do everything like an old 30s black and white movie – in a kind of slow motion. On the day your guests are to arrive, wake up at your leisure, take deep breaths, relax yourself, do everything slowly and purposefully. Amble downstairs, dribble the water into the kettle for that first cuppa, enjoy it, then face the day in an atmosphere of peace, tranquillity and organized hospitality. Only then will your mind turn to the little extra weekend comforts that you might just have forgotten: the stock of toilet paper in the bathroom, the 'hotties' for each bed if the weather is cold, the fresh flowers on the dressing tables.

There should never be any rigid schedules attached to a weekend (that's for weekdays only). Even if the timing of a meal goes slightly askew, does it really matter if you all sit down at a quarter to one or a quarter past one? If late, your guests will have had a further refill of booze; if early, they will probably find time and space for a cheap cooking brandy at the end of the meal to send them into the world of weekend, post-prandial snooze. None of the dishes in this book will suffer from ten minutes' extra time in the oven or on the hob (provided you turn the temperature down, of course) and by taking heed of this advice *you* will find yourself actually revelling in every minute of your time entertaining, and you will be glowing with pride at the praise showered on you. And why not, say I.

Gourmets and gourmands have come to associate Miller Howe with the best of haute cuisine, using the freshest of ingredients prepared in a masterly and unique way. Now here and now, put such thoughts out of your head. This is the Tovey *weekend* eating book. In come the cans of fish, the frozen peas, the shortcuts and extensive use of the freezer. In my private life at Willow Farm I often entertain on my weekly visits, and the finishing-off of partly-cooked dishes, the warming through of finished dishes all work extremely well. The critics may well raise their eyebrows and rush to sharpen their pencils to condemn but, believe you me, none of my guests have ever turned down or away from my ideas of weekend cooking. In fact, all go away happier and a few pounds heavier! Which is exactly how it should be.

Finally, I can only repeat that in no other aspect of cooking is common sense more necessary than in organizing during the week for the weekend. And, funnily enough, the purse doesn't seem to mind the odd few pence or so for additional meat or veg during the week: it all seems so much more economical than being confronted with an enormous Friday night supermarket basket and bill. And please note that, although I've divided the recipes into seven sections which should cover every possible weekend meal eventuality – breakfasts/brunches, light lunches, barbecues/picnics, afternoon teas, high teas, suppers, dinners and food gifts to take away – many of the recipes can be swapped around or tarted up to be relevant in another meal situation.

I hope my ideas will please you as much as they have pleased my guests – and me, as host. Enjoy your relaxing weekends!

BREAKFASTS AND BRUNCHES

As I firmly believe breakfasts and brunches should be just as much fun as other meals over the weekend, the first priority is a lack of flap over timing. Your guests are here to enjoy themselves, and if they've partaken of your generous hospitality the night before, they probably won't want you waking them at the crack of 8 or 9 a.m. to eat yet another meal. Breakfast dishes should be ones that can either have been pre-prepared – at least the night before – and that don't need cooking for too long when needed, or ones to which guests can help themselves. Selection of breakfast recipes should also depend on the season – the porridge, for instance, is ideal for a winter weekend – and on the programme for the rest of the day. Don't attempt a huge breakfast, lunch *and* dinner; a late brunch could be followed up by an afternoon tea and a dinner or supper, for instance. I think you'll find a fair old selection of recipes here from which to choose and select, and you shouldn't have to repeat an actual menu for several weeks – nay, months.

One of the things I do at home, whether at Brantlea or at Willow Farm, is to try to set up the table for breakfast the night before; in the conservatory attached to the kitchen at the latter, in the dining room upstairs at Brantlea (if we've used the conservatory downstairs for dinner the night before). This means I can get this task out of the way the afternoon before and therefore spend more time with my guests. The china, cutlery and glasses are all arranged, and the toaster is handy as are the tea and coffee pots. I have known some people look askance when I say that the dining table is set so far ahead, and I can see their clinical minds clicking away thinking of dust and germs. Obviously, at the farm, if I'm laying up the kitchen conservatory on a warm sultry night when the windows are wide open, I will put the cups on the saucers upside down, and likewise the glasses on the table. I also find those large mosquito net squares with beaded edges very useful. If you are a purist, you could simply drape the table with a clean, white sheet! However you might react to this idea, it does save so much time.

I also try to find the time the afternoon before to amass a collection of wild flowers and leaves when taking Ossie for a walk, and arrange them (well, plonk them) into a large jug. The simplest of buttercups, bluebells and wild grasses look wonderful on a breakfast table (although they become droopy quite quickly).

Another idea for guests who might be up at disparate hours is individual trays with teapots, cups, sugar, milk etc. Over the years I've been collecting that green, gold-trimmed French Apilco ware, and I've now got enough to lay up breakfast table *and* separate trays. If the guests wake early they can make their own tea or coffee – I have a huge selection of various types of tea from which they can choose – and indeed if they want to sneak something to eat then, they can make some toast: I leave a bread board out next to the bread tin holding both a white and a wholemeal (whole wheat) loaf. Those four- or six-slot commercial toasters – although on the pricey side – are a marvellous investment, especially if you are an enthusiastic or inveterate weekend entertainer. If it really is to be a self-service breakfast, you can leave out the sealed containers of muesli (granola) and various accompaniments, and tell your guests the night before the whereabouts of the milk and cream and the prepared fruit dishes such as the rhubarb, etc.

But *my* brunches – or late, lazy breakfasts as we call them in the north – are much more elaborate. I would be the first up to tidy downstairs and to set out the milks on the individual trays. I would gather together all the ingredients – mostly pre-prepared, of course – and set to organizing the latish breakfast. My guests might appear throughout these preparations, but they can take their teas or coffees back to their rooms, or to a quiet corner of the house to read the papers.

Buck's Fizz would definitely start the session off with style, using freshly squeezed orange juice and a sparkling white wine in equal proportions. The orange juice can have been made the night before and stored in an airtight container in the fridge, but it does lose a lot of its vitamins, and some of its flavour and sweetness. I would make this one of my first jobs, and the small electric juice extractors are very good indeed and not too expensive. I lay out an enormous piece of foil on my work surface with a wooden chopping board in the middle. I simply then slice the oranges in half through their equators and

Previous page: for a (nearly) healthy breakfast, try some Home-made Muesli (Granola) (page 14), followed by Rhubarb Cooked in Ginger Beer (page 16) and New Potatoes with Sour Cream and Keta (page 20).

press them down on the machine. I discard the debris on the foil, doing up to a dozen with ease (a good serving of orange juice usually needs *two* oranges), and then I remove the board and extractor, collect up all the skins in the foil and dump it in the wastebin.

Then, in the summer, I'd serve muesli (granola) with lots of soft brown sugar and yoghurt or perhaps some delicious English country honey. In the winter it would be the overnight porridge. The curried drop scones with smoked trout and horseradish cream with Keta (red caviar) could be the main course if you make sufficient scones, but I would prefer to serve this as a little appetizer most of the year, and then have something like the savoury mince (ground beef or lamb) topped with baked potato circles. I am a meat eater primarily and feel diddled if I don't have meat for lunch (in this case brunch, of course). I might finish off with the hot marmalade popovers, or with some freshly made toast, lots of butter and some home-made jam, marmalade or lemon curd (see page 154). On one occasion the combination of the new potatoes with sour cream and Keta (red caviar), followed by the braised ham steaks, seemed to go particularly well.

The main thing to remember about weekend breakfasts is the total relaxation of guests and of you as host/hostess. The food should be fun, delicious and easy to prepare – and you should enjoy it as much as them!

Passionate Figs with Brandy

A wonderfully exotic start to a summer breakfast. Make it the night before.

SERVES 6
12 fresh, ripe figs
6 fresh, ripe passionfruit
60 ml (4 tablespoons) brandy
30 ml (2 tablespoons) dry sherry
finely grated rind of 2 oranges
1 whole nutmeg, finely grated

Wipe the figs clean with a damp cloth then slit down two-thirds of the way from the top in a criss-cross. You want the cut sections to fall and fan out into four quarters, but still to be fixed by their uncut base. Halve the passionfruit and scoop the centre pulp and seeds out into a small bowl. Heat the brandy, sherry, orange rind and grated nutmeg together in a small saucepan.

Using a dish that will hold all the figs comfortably, uncut bottoms up, spread the passionfruit pulp on the base and put the figs into this, cut-side down. Pour over the warm alcoholic mixture and when cold, cover and chill overnight.

Home-made Muesli (Granola)

I am often appalled at what is sold commercially as muesli (granola), particularly those individual portions which seem to me to consist mostly of 99 per cent cereal and none of the other perks that should come with the dish.

I always make my own muesli, purchasing the cereal bases from the local health-food shop. These are mainly oats, barley, rye and wheat (both whole and cracked). To one or more of these, I add the following, according to what I have in the store cupboard, and to what takes my fancy: nuts, sultanas (white raisins), raisins, currants, chopped prunes, dried apple rings/peaches/pears/apricots/bananas (all coarsely chopped), lightly toasted pine kernels, and desiccated (shredded) coconut.

Everything is mixed well together in a bowl and then stored in airtight containers. As you can appreciate, this can have been done well in advance – weeks before, even – so all you have to do is get the containers out from which your guests can help themselves. Serve slices of fresh fruit or summer berries with the muesli, and offer runny honey and natural (plain) yoghurt as well as the more conventional sugar and milk.

Orange, Grapefruit and Lime Segments with Mint

An ideal way to start the day for those guests who are slightly apprehensive about eating too much and putting on any weight over their weekend. Nutritionists and foodies say that the acid in the fruit taken first thing in the morning burns up fat – so grin and bear it!

I usually serve this in a saucer champagne glass on a doyleyed, ferned and flowered plate to give it a bit of a 'lift' – and, best of all, it should be prepared the night before.

PER PERSON
1 grapefruit
1 orange
½ lime
a few sprigs of fresh mint

To segment the fruit, you need a very sharp serrated knife and a wooden work board. Cut off the stalk end and the base of the fruits to allow them to stand firm. Then, looking down at the circle of fresh fruit showing at the top, run the knife slowly downwards, removing a section of both pith and skin about 2.5 cm (1 inch) in width. This is quite easy provided you take it slowly the first time, and make sure you do expose the lovely juicy flesh. This will act as an excellent guide for you, inch by inch, to remove the whole of the skin and pith.

Put a plastic strainer (for catching the segments) over a bowl (for catching the juice) and then hold the skinned fruit in the palm of your hand, so that you can see the thin lines of membrane which lie between each segment. Go very, very carefully now as you simply run your knife ever so slowly along this membrane towards the middle of the fruit (when demonstrating this, I compare it to a bicycle wheel and you are running along the spokes towards the hub). If you do this on the inside of each segment, they soon fall out into the sieve and the juice passes through into the bowl underneath. Sounds awfully complicated and at first it is – but oh, so worth all the trouble.

Thereafter, once you have segmented everything, mix the segments together and store overnight in an airtight container. Store the juice separately as the segments would go slightly soggy if left in it. In the morning, either serve the juice as a drink in small sherry glasses, or pour over the fruit in a serving dish. Garnish with fresh sprigs of garden mint.

Overnight Porridge

Use a double saucepan for this, or a large bowl that fits snugly into a saucepan.

SERVES 6
105 ml (6 heaped tablespoons)
   porridge (rolled) oats
a pinch of salt
900 ml (1½ pints/3¾ cups) warmed
   milk
TO SERVE
soft brown sugar, butter and malt
   whisky

The night before, put the porridge oats, salt and warmed milk into a bowl over a pan or into the top half of a double boiler. Half fill the base part with boiling water, and put in a warm place – an oven with a lit pilot light, the plate-warming drawer of your switched-off oven after you have finished cooking, or a lovely warm airing cupboard. Leave overnight.

In the morning, simply stir the contents, then put on the stove over the double-boiler or saucepan base, and cook for 10 minutes. Serve with a little soft brown sugar, a knob of butter and a dash of malt whisky.

Rhubarb Cooked in Ginger Beer

This rhubarb dish is ideal for breakfast, but any leftovers can be served with ice cream or custard, or puréed to go as a small dollop alongside many meat dishes. It can be made a couple of days in advance and stored in the fridge.

SERVES 6
900 g (2 lb) fresh rhubarb
butter
2 small bottles ginger beer

There are some fanatics who say rhubarb should always be peeled, and others who say leave all the skin on. Personally I like to compromise, and after having wiped each stick clean with a damp cloth, I take strips of skin off to give a striped-awning effect. What is important, however, is that each stick should be cut into the same size pieces – mine are normally about 7.5 cm (3 inch) long – and you should always discard the leaves and whitish base.

Grease the base of your cooking dish – which should measure about 27.5 × 32.5 cm (11 × 13 inch) – with butter. Place the rhubarb pieces in the dish and pour the ginger beer over them. There is no need to cover the dish. Cook in a preheated oven at 180°C/350°F/ mark 4 for 10–15 minutes for firmish but edible rhubarb; for 15–20 minutes for a slightly softer texture; and for 25 minutes for rhubarb for toothless geriatrics! Cover and put it in the fridge when cool.

Scrambled Eggs

Scrambled eggs usually have to be done at the very last minute with your guests sitting down with knives and forks ready to start the attack. But by doing them this way, you can cook two-thirds of the way (about 35 minutes) through and put to one side. Then, when everyone has finished the starter, you can proceed with the cooking (another 10 minutes) whilst somebody else makes the toast and coffee.

SERVES 6
15 eggs
generous amounts of freshly
  ground black pepper
5 ml (1 teaspoon) salt
75 ml (5 tablespoons) milk
45 ml (3 tablespoons) double
  (heavy) cream

The first necessity is a very large heatproof bowl to hold all those eggs (on the generous side, I know, but it's a *brunch* dish you're preparing). This bowl should rest gently in a large saucepan of simmering water, but the water must *not* touch the base or sides of the bowl.

Put all the ingredients apart from the cream into the bowl. When the water is boiling put the bowl on the saucepan and leave for 20 minutes.

Have ready an electric hand-held whisk to beat the eggs, but a stainless steel wire whisk will suffice. Remove the bowl from the pan (you will need to add a little hot water to replenish that which has 'steamed' away) and beat the living daylights out of your eggs. Return to the pan and leave for a further 15 minutes. You can stop here and wait for however long is necessary.

When you and guests are ready to eat, the eggs take 10 minutes to heat through and finish off. Remove from the heat and beat in the cream.

Serve as they are with triangles of toast or, better still, some horrendously fattening (but ever so good) croûtons. However, if you wish to amplify the eggs even further, small cubes of smoked salmon or flakes of smoked trout may be added and, of course, a can of Keta (red caviar) is marvellous. Apart from looking so pretty, as each single ball of roe bursts in your mouth it explodes with a release of richly flavoured oil!

Overleaf: for an exotic breakfast, serve Passionate Figs with Brandy (page 14), then follow with Curried Drop Scones with Smoked Trout, Horseradish Cream and Keta (page 25).

Poached Eggs

The easiest way to poach eggs is in a large, round, not very deep saucepan (I use a deep-lipped frying pan). Fill it two-thirds with cold water and a touch of wine vinegar. Bring to the boil, turn down to simmering and then break your egg in.

Immediately, with a long-handled spoon, 'mould' the egg into an oval shape. The egg is cooked when the transparent mass is totally white. Use the large spoon to gently remove it to a tray lined with two or three thicknesses of kitchen paper towels to dry it. Transfer thereafter to your circle or square of hot buttered toast.

New Potatoes with Sour Cream and Keta

I use Keta a lot. This is the trade name of American red salmon caviar roe, which is made from the eggs of the keta or dog salmon which spawns in Siberian and Canadian rivers flowing into the Pacific. Thus it's not real *caviar (the eggs of the sturgeon), but it is delicious, with huge red bubbles.*

SERVES 6

550 g (1¼ lb) small new potatoes
10 ml (2 teaspoons) salt
5 ml (1 teaspoon) fresh lemon
   juice
50 g (2 oz/4 tablespoons) soft
   butter
150 ml (¼ pint/⅔ cup) sour cream
100 g (4 oz) Keta
sprigs of fresh parsley

What is important about this dish is that you should have new potatoes of exactly the same size. I normally dig around for those about the size of a walnut. Don't peel them as the flavour is very much in the skin. I simply brush them with a nailbrush which I keep for this task alone, the bristles of which I've cut down to about 6 mm (¼ inch) deep. As the potatoes are scrubbed, pop them into a pan containing 600 ml (1 pint) water. Add the salt, lemon juice and butter and put the pan on the hob. Bring to the boil and cook for about 5 minutes (longer, of course, if they're larger than walnuts).

Strain them and return immediately to the saucepan. Shake for a few seconds over heat to dry off any liquid and put to one side. When cool enough to handle, slice thin strips off two opposing sides so that each potato can lie relatively flat and has a surface to be coated. (Slice larger potatoes in half.) Leave to become cold.

Just before serving, put some sour cream on top of each potato and a teaspoon of Keta.

Savoury Custards

These basically consist of a quiche filling without the pastry which means you neither have the fag of making the pastry nor are you ingesting all those pastry calories. (However, between you and I, I reckon each portion represents even more filling than a generous portion of pastry quiche!) I can remember having something similar to this at the Michelin-starred restaurant Au Vieux Port in Le Lavandou one rather wet, miserable day. The chef, Denis le Cadre, had made an egg custard in a fluted flan dish with the most tasty mussels I have ever come across, and it was served on a wickedly rich, mushroom cream sauce. With each mouthful I continually assured myself that there was no pastry to add to the calories, and on the first Sunday I was home I did a similar dish using off-cuts of smoked salmon. I was very popular with my house guests for the rest of the day!

The ramekins can be buttered and seasoned the night before, but I would leave the actual mixing of the custard until the morning. It doesn't take long.

SERVES 6

450 ml ($\frac{3}{4}$ pint/2 cups) double (heavy) cream

3 eggs plus 1 egg yolk

a pinch of salt

a touch of grated nutmeg

a generous grind of black pepper

FILLING

100–175 g (4–6 oz) flaked smoked trout or diced smoked salmon

or

150 g (5 oz) mushroom pâté (see page 149)

or

50 g (2 oz/$\frac{1}{2}$ cup) bacon, chopped, with 50 g (2 oz/$\frac{1}{2}$ cup) grated cheese and 3 tomatoes, skinned, pipped and chopped

or

6 chicken livers, cleaned and chopped, with 12 walnuts and the finely grated rind of 1 orange

Mix the cream, eggs, egg yolk and seasonings well together and divide evenly between the six greased and seasoned ramekins. Divide one of the fillings into six portions and pop into the custards. Place the filled ramekins in a roasting tray (pan) and preheat the oven to 190°C/375°F/mark 5. Pour enough boiling water into the roasting tray to come up at least half-way up the sides of each ramekin, and place the tray in the oven. Cook for 30–35 minutes. Bring them out of the oven and allow to cool for about 3–5 minutes (beware of draughts). Serve on a doyleyed, ferned plate with a teaspoon – eat out of the ramekin – and accompany with toast or well buttered slices of brown bread.

If you have a fan oven, I feel sorry for you as egg custards seem to rise like soufflés during cooking and then fall back leaving a rather thickish skin and sad deflated dish. One can slightly overcome this tragedy by covering the whole cooking dish with foil and lowering the temperature to 180°C/350°F/mark 4. Cook for the same amount of time.

Overleaf: for a weekend breakfast in bed, serve some Orange, Grapefruit and Lime Segments with Mint (page 15), and home-made Fish Cakes (page 24).

Fish Cakes

Some people turn up their noses at such simple fare, but when they are prepared lavishly they are a real joy. Once again they can be prepared during the week from extra fish you might purchase for a meal, and popped into the freezer.

MAKES 6
basic fishy ingredients of choice
(see below)
225 g (8 oz) potatoes, peeled
salt
2 eggs
plain (all-purpose) flour
SAVOURY BREADCRUMBS
75 g (3 oz/1¾ cups) fine fresh
breadcrumbs
25 g (1 oz) Cheddar cheese, finely
grated
8 ml (½ tablespoon) very finely
chopped parsley
a tiny pinch of English (dry)
mustard powder

To prepare the potato part of the fish cake, cut the potatoes into even-sized pieces and boil until soft with a pinch of salt. Strain and then return to the pan to dry off over heat. Separate one of the eggs, and add the yolk to the potatoes. Mash with a fork or masher until really creamy, and then pass through a rough sieve to make sure there are no lumps of starch lurking around. Divide into six equal portions when cold.

Beat the remaining egg and the egg whites together and put on a plate. Flour your work surface and mix the ingredients for the savoury breadcrumbs together on another plate. Mix together the fishy ingredients of choice, then divide into six portions. Mix each portion with a portion of mashed potato.

Clean hands are now essential as you need to mould each fish cake into a ball and then flatten into circles on the floured work surface. Sprinkle more flour on top. Paint each fish cake with beaten egg wash and coat with the savoury breadcrumbs. Lay out flat on a baking tray, cover and chill, or pile up with greaseproof between each one, wrap in foil and freeze.

To cook the fish cakes, bring round to room temperature, and simply fry them in butter or oil until they're brown, turning them once, about 10–15 minutes. Drain well before serving.

Crab with Sweetcorn (Corn on the Cob)

350 g (12 oz) white crab meat, flaked
50 g (2 oz/½ cup) sweetcorn (corn on the cob)
kernels, cooked
5 ml (1 teaspoon) English (dry) mustard
powder
15 ml (1 tablespoon) fresh chopped parsley
a pinch of salt
a touch of finely grated nutmeg or mace

White Fish with Red (Bell) Pepper, Grated Courgette (Zucchini) and Lime

350 g (12 oz) poached white fish, flaked
1 red (bell) pepper, washed, seeded and diced
50 g (2 oz) courgettes (zucchini), coarsely
grated into the juice of ½ fresh lime

Salmon, Fennel and Dill

350 g (12 oz) cooked salmon, boned and flaked

50 g (2 oz) fennel bulb, finely chopped

30 ml (2 tablespoons) coarsely snipped dill

Tuna, Pea and Onion

350 g (12 oz) canned tuna, drained and flaked

50 g (2 oz/$\frac{1}{2}$ cup) frozen peas, defrosted

25 g (1 oz) onion, peeled and finely chopped

Curried Drop Scones with Smoked Trout, Horseradish Cream and Keta

Whenever I visit New York I try to have a quick lunch in the Russian Tea Room with my long-standing friend, Rosemary, where we always order the buckwheat pancakes with sour cream and Keta (red caviar). It is a lovely, slow, ritual buttering each pancake, then spreading the soured cream topping with the delightful, delicious, mouth-watering, rich bubbles of roe whilst catching up on the news and gossip . . . . But down to earth. This is my less traditional, more substantial alternative for breakfast.

MAKES 18 SCONES

225 g (8 oz/1$\frac{1}{2}$ cups) self-raising (self-rising) flour

$\frac{1}{2}$ teaspoon salt

1 teaspoon curry powder of choice

50 g (2 oz/3 tablespoons) caster (superfine) sugar

50 g (2 oz/4 tablespoons) soft butter

2 eggs

10 tablespoons milk

FILLING AND TOPPING

300 ml ($\frac{1}{2}$ pint/1$\frac{1}{4}$ cups) double (heavy) cream, whipped

1 teaspoon horseradish cream

100 g (4 oz) smoked trout, finely flaked

100 g (4 oz) Keta

Mix all the dry ingredients together in a mixing bowl and then gently rub in half the butter. Beat the eggs and milk together. Make a well in the middle of the flour and add the liquid, stirring the flour slowly in, until you have a smooth paste mixture. Beat with an electric hand-held mixer for about 2–3 minutes, and then leave to one side, covered, for about 15 minutes.

You should have a griddle pan for this but a heavy-bottomed frying pan (skillet) will suffice. Heat the pan and paint some of the remaining butter, melted, over the surface. Drop off 4 separate dessertspoons ($\frac{3}{4}$ tablespoons) of the mixture – allowing room around each dollop – and as soon as the base is cooked, flip each scone over with a palette knife and cook until fairly firm. As the scones come off the griddle, place them between the folds of a clean teatowel to keep warm.

For the filling and topping, remove half of the whipped cream from the bowl. Put it in a piping bag with a star nozzle. Fold the horseradish cream and flaked smoked trout into the balance in the bowl and use this mixture to form a sandwich filling between two of the cooked drop scones, and then pipe the plain cream on top. Garnish with a teaspoon of Keta.

Savoury Beef or Lamb topped with Baked Potato Circles

The savoury mince can have been made in advance and frozen; the little dishes can be put together the night before and kept in the fridge.

SERVES 6

675 g (1½ lb) savoury mince
 (ground beef or lamb) (see
 page 118)
butter
6 potatoes, peeled, parboiled and
 thinly sliced

Divide the savoury mince evenly between six well buttered ramekins. Spread the potato slices over the meat in overlapping layers, and each time you put a potato slice down paint it with melted butter. Go round in a circle until all the potato is used up. Cover the dishes and leave until needed.

In a preheated oven at 190°C/375°F/mark 5 they take 30 minutes to cook well through and for the potatoes to become beautifully crisp and brown. Serve with home-made chutneys (see pages 152–4).

Marmalade Popovers

The batter for these can be made the night before and finished off next morning when the olive oil is beaten in. If timed well, they can be such a marvellous climax to the simplest of breakfasts. They are like Yorkshire puddings really, and you could use lemon curd (see page 154) or jam instead of the marmalade.

MAKES 8 POPOVERS

100 g (4 oz/¾ cup) strong plain
 (hard all purpose) flour
a pinch of salt
a touch of freshly grated nutmeg
2 eggs, lightly beaten with 150 ml
 (¼ pint/⅔ cup) cold milk and
 45 ml (3 tablespoons) single
 (light) cream
15 ml (1 tablespoon) good olive
 oil
120 ml (8 teaspoons) marmalade
 (one for every popover)

Sieve the flour, salt and nutmeg into a bowl and make a well in the middle. Into this pour the egg/milk/cream mixture and slowly combine, using an electric hand-held whisk, until you have a bubbling batter. Cover with a teatowel and leave in a very cool place overnight.

The next morning, preheat the oven to 220°C/425°F/mark 7. Remove the teatowel from the bowl and beat in the olive oil. Oil some of those trays for small Victorian sponge cakes – which normally come with nine or twelve compartments – and put in the oven to get really hot. Then, allowing 25 minutes' cooking time, ladle the mixture into the heated trays, letting it come about two-thirds up the side of each 'cup'. Spoon a teaspoon of marmalade into the centre of each pop-over. Place immediately in the oven and leave until cooked, when they should be very crisp and puffy.

I like to sprinkle them with sieved icing (confectioners') sugar, and do make sure your guests have very large napkins as sometimes the marmalade 'explodes', which can make for a messy breakfast!

Kidneys in Cream with Port Wine and Croûtons

Kidneys go a little tough if they're prepared too long in advance of cooking, so make this dish at the last minute. It takes very little time though – and it's delicious. You can serve the kidneys, as here, in ramekins, but they could also be served in a ring of mashed potato or in a pastry casing of some sort.

For a change, you could cook the kidneys in exactly the same way as below, but using 350 g (12 oz) instead of 450 g (1 lb), and 150 ml ($\frac{1}{4}$ pint/$\frac{2}{3}$ cup) of an inexpensive claret instead of the reduced port and cream. Add 175 g (6 oz/3 cups) of chopped mushroom caps with the wine, and a pinch of English (dry) mustard powder could be sprinkled into the pan with the flour for extra tang.

SERVES 6

160 ml (12 tablespoons) port wine

300 ml ($\frac{1}{2}$ pint/1$\frac{1}{4}$ cups) double (heavy) cream

100 g (4 oz/$\frac{1}{2}$ cup) butter

225 g (8 oz) onions, peeled and finely diced

450 g (1 lb) lamb's kidneys, skinned, fibres and cores removed

a little plain (all-purpose) flour from your flour shaker

6 croûtons

Start by preparing the sauce. You need two small saucepans – one for the port and one for the cream. Put these into the saucepans and reduce each by half, taking good care not to go beyond this point. Combine both together and whisk lightly.

Meanwhile, melt the butter in a large frying pan (skillet) and fry the onion until nice and golden. Roughly chop the kidneys into even-sized pieces about the size of your thumb-nail. Add to the cooked onion and cook for 2 minutes over a high heat. Sprinkle with a little flour and cook for a further 2 minutes.

Pour the sauce over the cooked kidneys and onion, and portion out into warmed ramekins. Serve with warmed croûtons, and have freshly ground pepper available on the table.

Bacon Chops in Wine, with Curried Stuffed Apples

Both the chops and the stuffed apples can be prepared the night before, but paint all the cut surfaces of the apples — both slices and the whole ones to be stuffed — with lemon juice to prevent discoloration.

SERVES 6

6 bacon chops, at least 2 cm
 ($\frac{3}{4}$ inch) thick, weighing about
 1.6 kg ($3\frac{1}{2}$ lb) in total

450 ml ($\frac{3}{4}$ pint/2 cups) dry white
 wine or cider (hard cider)

15 ml (1 tablespoon) seasoned
 flour

50 g (2 oz/4 tablespoons) butter

7 Granny Smith apples

75 g (3 oz) onions, peeled and
 finely chopped

75 g (3 oz/$\frac{1}{2}$ cup) sultanas (white
 raisins) (preferably plumped
 overnight in brandy)

75 g (3 oz) breadcrumbs

7.5 ml ($1\frac{1}{2}$ teaspoons) curry
 powder of choice

You get a much better result, both in taste and texture, if you marinate your chops in the wine (or cider) for 2–3 days, covered, in the fridge. Thereafter dry them well, coat with the seasoned flour, and seal and brown them in the butter.

Remove from the pan and, when they're cool enough to handle, make an incision about two-thirds along the skin of the chops into the flesh itself, to make a little cavity. Peel, quarter, core and thinly slice one of the apples, and divide the slices between the six chop cavities. Push them in well.

When you want to cook, place the chops and wine in an ovenproof dish or roasting tin (approximately 30 × 35 cm/12 × 14 inch), cover with foil, and cook in the preheated oven at 180°C/350°F/mark 4 for 40 minutes.

Meanwhile, prepare the curried stuffed apples. Wipe the six remaining apples with a damp cloth and, using a sharp pointed knife, cut in from the stalk end down towards the bottom of the core, scooping out a triangular wedge. This cone-shaped cavity is where the stuffing will go. Using the butter in which you fried the chops, fry the onion until golden brown, then fold in the sultanas, breadcrumbs and curry powder. When cool, fill the apples, heaping the filling up on top. Put the stuffed apples into a suitable cooking container and add 2 tablespoons water. Cover with kitchen foil and place in the oven beside the chops for 15 minutes. Serve on hot plates.

Braised Ham Steak with Pineapple and Herb Topping and Baked Egg

SERVES 6

6 ham steaks, about 2 cm ($\frac{3}{4}$ inch)
   thick, weighing approx. 1.4 kg
   (3 lb) in total

300 ml ($\frac{1}{2}$ pint) white wine

6 slices fresh pineapple, peeled
   and cored, about 6 mm ($\frac{1}{4}$ inch)
   thick

50 g (2 oz/4 tablespoons) butter,
   melted

freshly chopped herbs

6 small eggs

4 tablespoons double (heavy)
   cream (optional)

about 50 g (2 oz) Cheddar cheese,
   finely grated (optional)

As with the bacon chops, these steaks are much better if left to marinate for 2–3 days in the wine in a covered dish in the fridge. Turn them periodically.

When you want to cook them, preheat the oven to 180°C/350°F/mark 4, place the steaks in the ovenproof dish (or a roasting tin) with the wine, cover with kitchen foil, and braise for 40 minutes. Meanwhile, quickly sear the pineapple slices in the melted butter.

Remove the ham steaks from the oven and pour off the winey juices into a small saucepan. Place the cooked pineapple rings over each of the ham steaks and sprinkle with herbs – any you may have which appeal to your palate – and then break a small egg into the circle of each pineapple, allowing the white to trail over the edges. Return to the oven, and the egg will take 8–10 minutes to cook, depending on how you like your yolk done.

Meanwhile, if you would like a sauce, put the saucepan with the winey juices in it over a high heat and reduce by half. Add the cream to this if you are feeling very wicked and couldn't care less about calories. Alternatively, half-way through the cooking of the egg, the dish can be removed from the oven, the eggs coated with the grated cheese, and the whole 'flashed' under a very hot grill (broiler).

Overleaf: a more substantial breakfast or brunch, consisting of a Bacon Chop in Wine with a Curried Stuffed Apple (opposite), Marmalade Popovers (page 26), and fresh orange juice.

LIGHT LUNCHES, PICNICS AND BARBECUES

Apart from Sunday lunch, which I like to be splendidly traditional (see the Dinners section for a selection of three-course meals which could be served as more substantial lunches), I tend to think in terms of lighter meals in the middle of the day. I will have served a good breakfast, might be considering offering an afternoon tea – and I always (if there is no conflicting arrangement) like to serve a glamorous and exciting dinner. So a light, less formal meal is by far the most appropriate. It could be served in the kitchen, or the garden if the weather is good enough. Many of the same dishes could be taken on a walk or a picnic, or to the beach where you might have a barbecue.

Once again the emphasis is on pre-preparation, and many of the recipes can be made up at least the night before, or earlier in the week and frozen. Seasonal lunches at home are no problem – and the other sections of the book can be scoured for equally suitable recipes (like the cheese pastry tartlets on page 141 or the cauliflower cheese on page 112) – but moveable feasts require a great deal more organization and thought.

Packers of picnics usually fall into one of two camps – mainly Melamine (plastic) or mostly Meissen – and I find myself half-way between the two! I possess an all-purpose-built wicker picnic hamper, but I must admit it spends most of its time languishing in the attic for whilst it looks very luxurious, it is so impractical. The two large square Melamine (plastic) boxes always seem the wrong size for the main course I plan to serve, and the time spent putting everything back into its allotted place does try my patience the following day (rather like doing a jigsaw puzzle). What I prefer is an enormous wicker basket with a handle, which I line with a large red and white gingham cloth. (I have another which I simply fold in four to cover all the contents of the basket when full along with, of course, some matching napkins.) I have collected airtight containers of all shapes and sizes over the years, and I never throw away any jar that has a tight-fitting screw-top lid as they're excellent for carrying cream, sauces, chutney, French dressing or mayonnaise etc. I have lots of that lovely 'bubble' paper – the sort that encases ornaments when purchased from good stores – and this is used to interleave the good pieces of china (otherwise save good strong tissue paper through the year for picnic parties).

The cutlery (flatware) I take along in its canteen (a curious word this, for cutlery stored in these boxes is seldom the sort found in such as a works' canteen!). Don't forget to take along a large container with lid for all the dirty cutlery to be popped into when packing up. And I never go to have a meal in the open air without taking a large plastic bag containing a face (wash) cloth for each guest; these have been soaked in boiling water, had some after-shave sprinkled on, and then squeezed almost dry – you have no idea how messy one can get when eating out of doors! The strong plastic cool boxes are ideal for the booze and anything which requires to be kept cool – but, a few days prior to the picnic, keep stockpiling ice cubes into a container in the freezer so that you have an abundance. I take proper glasses which look best, but you can buy very smart-looking plastic glasses made in Italy (broken glass in the countryside is a menace to all and sundry). A large sheet of very strong plastic is put down on the ground you find to use as your base, and then this is covered with travelling rugs (don't forget a few cushions too). When travelling by car to a picnic, always travel *cluttered* so that you cosset yourself throughout the day. (I must admit I always have a good old giggle to myself when I time and time again see folk picnicking in lay-bys at the side of extremely busy main roads. The car boot is opened, portable table and chairs unloaded and erected, and they sit there sipping and eating, breathing in carbon monoxide rather than clean country air. They always seem to be well content and happy, though, which only goes to show that it doesn't take much to please some.)

Obviously if you're going on a walking picnic, you'll not want to be overladen, so choose food that will travel well and won't easily be squashed or broken. The turnovers, for instance, are ideal, but if you've got a good rucksack, you could take a variety of other things, such as crudités and dips, and a thermos of 'cowboy' coffee.

Don't forget, whatever type of picnic that you're going on, that salads travel well, packed in an airtight container. Carry the dressing separately in a screw-top jar. Fresh fruit, too, is often much more portable than a made pudding – although sponges filled with cream or lemon curd wrap well in clingfilm (plastic wrap), whole or in wedges.

If you're going on a picnic barbecue, I find the inexpensive portable barbecues a boon, as all you have to find is a flat piece of ground to erect it on (none of that searching around, often in vain, for enough wood to get a fire going). Take ample barbecue coals and, more important still, a bottle of fast-firing liquid – but get the non-smelling sort, otherwise everything tastes of meths. Using this miraculous liquid a barbecue can be on its way in 5 minutes and ready to be used in about 20.

Plates, cutlery, cloths, ground sheets, 'home' comforts, etc. can all be the same as for a picnic – and of course you could go for more traditional barbecue meats – steaks, chops, chicken portions or meat kebabs. These should all have been marinated for days before in a good marinade for the best flavour and maximum tenderness. I can't be bothered being ultra polite and actually cooking all the meats for everybody. "How do you like yours, Hilda? Medium rare, or pink in the middle with a charred outside?" Let them all do their own, so take along a few pairs of tongs. There is nothing quite like the smell and taste of charcoal-grilled meats, and try to take some dried (or fresh) rosemary to scatter over the coals (particularly for lamb or pork). Foil packages are practical and fun – the quail and trout, for instance – but lack a degree of thrill. However, they can be plonked on and left while you go in for your first swim!

At the end of the barbecue, when you are full of all those lovely meats, barbecued marshmallows is a very childish – but moreish – dish, and one I never tire of. I simply thread two or three bought marshmallows (better here than my home-made ones, see page 80!), on to a skewer and toast them over the dying embers. They become rather tacky (some even say sickly) and are decidedly decadent . . . .

Don't forget the oven gloves for dismantling the barbecue and a bucket for fetching the water to dowse the fire and cool everything down prior to packing back into the boot of the car.

Quick Tomato and Basil Soup with Grated Cheese

Take this soup on a picnic in a good thermos flask. Carry the cheese separately.

SERVES 6
100 g (4 oz/$\frac{1}{2}$ cup) butter
225 g (8 oz) onions, peeled and
   finely chopped
1.4 kg (3 lb) ripe tomatoes, wiped,
   stalks *on*
150 ml ($\frac{1}{4}$ pint/$\frac{2}{3}$ cup) sherry
6–8 fresh basil leaves
TO SERVE
Lancashire or Cheddar cheese,
   grated

Melt the butter in a saucepan and cook the onion until golden. Add the tomatoes, sherry and basil leaves, cover with a double thickness of dampened greaseproof (wax) paper, and simmer for 30 minutes, covered.

Liquidize, pass through a sieve, and when cold, chill or even freeze (in ice-cube trays, turned out into plastic bags, and reheated if still frozen in a bowl over a pan of simmering water).

Be generous with the cheese when you serve the steaming soup in individual bowls: a Cheddar is good, but a Lancashire is infinitely better.

Savoury Mushroom Caps

If you want to take these on a barbecue or picnic, wrap each little 'open sandwich' individually in foil, and heat through over the coals.

SERVES 6
36 mushroom caps (at least
  5 cm/2 inch across), peeled
about 100 g (4 oz/$\frac{1}{2}$ cup) butter
6 large thin slices bread, toasted
Bovril (Miso)
STUFFING
100 g (4 oz) onions, peeled and
   finely chopped
350 g (12 oz) sausagemeat (bulk
   sausage)
1 egg
30 ml (2 tablespoons) (at least)
   finely chopped parsley
1 garlic clove, crushed (optional)
10 ml (2 teaspoons) English (dry)
   mustard powder
15 ml (1 tablespoon) tomato
   purée (paste)

Make the stuffing first. Melt 25 g (1 oz/1$\frac{1}{2}$ tablespoons) of the butter and cook the onion until golden. Add the sausagemeat with the rest of the ingredients and simmer, stirring from time to time, for 20 minutes. Leave to go cold.

You won't be able to get all the mushrooms into your frying pan (skillet) at one go, so fry them in two stages. Use about half the butter for each stage, but leave a little to spread thinly on the toast. Cook until the mushrooms brown, then leave them to drain.

Cut out large fluted croûton shapes from the toasted bread slices. Spread the remaining butter over them and then, very sparsely, colour them with some Bovril. Divide the cooked stuffing into 18 balls and force these between two mushroom caps (to form a 'ball sandwich'). Arrange three on each croûton, and arrange these in turn on a baking tray (or in foil for a barbecue).

When you wish to cook the mushrooms, heat through for 15 minutes at 180°C/350°F/mark 4.

Crudités and Dips

Once upon a time, in smart trendy restaurants, it was fashionable to dunk sticks of celery, carrot and pepper (bell pepper) into bought mayonnaise flavoured with bought tomato sauce as you browsed through the menu or wine list. Done well, though, in substantial quantities and with a variety of good, home-made and imaginative dips, they can be an effective start to a meal. If at home, I spend a little time preparing six individual plates of the cut vegetables, and then put two sets of dips on the table so that three people can each dabble in a bowl to their hearts' content. (Which always reminds me of those once fashionable fondue parties where my long-handled stabber always seemed to get entwined with somebody else's or my piece of meat floated away or emerged uncooked. Towards the end of the evening I would tend to eat the meat virtually raw just to get some form of substance to balance the booze intake. I'm glad those days are over.)

Back to the vegetable crudités. It is important that you should have each stick more or less the same size. You need a good sharp knife, a wooden board . . . and patience. Round root vegetables such as swede (rutabaga), turnip, celeriac (celery root) and kohlrabi (the latter not really a root vegetable as it forms just above ground level) need to be peeled and then cut into even-sized thick circles. Pile these circles up two or three at a time and then cut them into chip-sized pieces (keep all the odd bits to be made into a cream of vegetable soup).

To prepare your red, green and yellow (bell) peppers simply wipe with a damp cloth, slice through lengthwise, and get rid of the stalk and seeds. Wash under slow running cold water and cut each half into equal thick strips. Cut wiped cucumbers lengthwise then remove the pips using a teaspoon; cut the halves into chunks and then into strips. (Don't ever remove the skin as they become quite soggy.) Celery is prepared in a similar fashion. Large mushroom caps should be skinned and then sliced and re-assembled to form the centre of your serving plate – topped with a radish flower possibly? A whole fennel bulb chopped in half provides from its centre some lovely fennel 'scoops' with light green furry tops. Carrots and parsnips are peeled, cut lengthwise into pieces, and then cut into sticks.

Use iceberg lettuce with its extremely strong leaf as a base on which to start arranging your colourful galaxy of strips; divide each veg from its neighbour with lots of watercress heads, parsley or other herb leaves, all of which can be eaten and look attractive. Cover the plate with clingfilm (plastic wrap) and keep somewhere cool prior to serving. If you're going on a picnic, wrap the individual bunches of veg strips in clingfilm.

As for the dips, a food processor or liquidizer is the essential piece of equipment for making them smooth and creamy, and although it does have to be cleaned after each separate combination has been put in, it is still an easy task! I must admit I don't actually wash mine between each dip mixing, but simply wipe it with kitchen paper. Inevitably I don't get into every nook and cranny, but a little of the previous dip mixed with the one you are now doing isn't going to harm anything or anybody.

Try some of the following combinations – and if you're going to take them on a picnic, put them in those little containers with see-through lids.

1. 2 avocado pears with 15 ml (3 teaspoons) horseradish cream and the juice and rind of $\frac{1}{2}$ lemon.

2. 3 large tomatoes, skinned and seeded, with 25 g (1 oz/1$\frac{1}{2}$ tablespoons) chopped celery, 1 skinned, cored and chopped apple, 12 ml (1 dessertspoon/$\frac{3}{4}$ tablespoon) tomato purée (paste) and 5 ml (1 teaspoon) Worcestershire sauce.

3. 175 g (6 oz) leftover Stilton cheese with 45 ml (3 tablespoons) inexpensive port wine.

4. 175 g (6 oz/1$\frac{1}{2}$ cups) cooked peas with 1 peeled cored pear, and a bunch of watercress. Fold in a bunch of finely chopped spring onions (scallions).

Once again, you will frequently find leftover items in the fridge (pâté, terrines, stuffings) that will come together with some flavouring, apricot jam, chutney or spiced jellies being used as a binding. Thick Greek yoghurt can also be used with toasted sesame seeds or pine kernels, a touch of curry powder or your favourite chutney, and I like to add finely crushed dried banana flakes. Leftover bacon should be baked until quite firm and then crushed with a rolling pin between kitchen paper. These bits combined with peanut butter make a delicious dip. And finally, for real pigginess (and why not?) dripping and jelly from a roast can be used with some savoury breadcrumbs (see page 24) for a thicker texture.

Overleaf: for a picnic lunch, start with Tomato and Basil Soup (page 35) and Mini Wheatmeal Loaves (page 69), and then tuck into a Wheatmeal Quiche (page 56) – here made with peppers – and a radicchio salad with pecans.

Savoury Cheese Balls

These 'coloured' balls are very versatile. They could be served as a cheese course at lunch or dinner, but I often serve them as a starter with crisp lettuce, radish flowers dipped in sea salt, and celery twirls (a glass of inexpensive red wine served slightly chilled goes well too!). Serve three on individual plates, one of each colour. You could roll plain cream cheese in other substances for different colours, tastes and textures – toasted fine (instant) oatmeal, for instance, or toasted sesame seeds.

If you want to take these on a picnic, they will have to be packed in a firm box and kept in one of those portable freezer bags or chill boxes.

EACH RECIPE MAKES 6 BALLS

Orange Cheese Balls

100 g (4 oz/1 cup) very good, full-fat cream cheese
juice and finely grated rind of ½ orange
about 50 g (2 oz/½ cup) flaked almonds, toasted

For the Orange Cheese Balls: place the cream cheese in your food processor (or a small bowl and use an electric hand-held whisk), and beat in the orange juice and rind. Divide mixture into six and shape each into a ball. Roll in the toasted flaked almonds and leave to become firm, covered with clingfilm (plastic wrap), in the fridge.

Cheese and Herb Balls

100 g (4 oz/1 cup) cheese and herb pâté (see page 148)
very finely chopped fresh herbs

For the Cheese and Herb Balls: simply make into six balls as above and then roll in the herbs. Chill.

Stilton, Port and Walnut Balls

100 g (4 oz/1 cup) leftover Stilton
8 ml (½ tablespoon) double (heavy) cream
15 ml (1 tablespoon) port wine
50 g (2 oz/⅓ cup) walnuts, coarsely chopped

For the Stilton, Port and Walnut Balls: mix the Stilton, cream and port in a food processor until nice and smooth. Make into six balls and roll them in the chopped walnuts. Chill.

Chilled Jellied Poussin (Rock Cornish Hen)

This dish must be cooked the day before you want to eat it, and because it sets to a jelly, it is ideal fare for a picnic if travelling by car — nothing slops over the side of the casserole dish as you go over the bumps!

SERVES 6

300 ml ($\frac{1}{2}$ pint/1$\frac{1}{4}$ cups) chicken stock

300 ml ($\frac{1}{2}$ pint/1$\frac{1}{4}$ cups) dry white wine

150 ml ($\frac{1}{4}$ pint/$\frac{2}{3}$ cup) dry sherry

15 g ($\frac{1}{2}$ oz) powdered gelatine

25 g (1 oz/2 tablespoons) butter

100 g (4 oz) onions, peeled and finely chopped

225 g (8 oz) assorted root vegetables (turnips, parsnips, carrots), peeled and chopped

3 baby poussins (Rock Cornish hens), about 400 g (14 oz) each

2 small pig's trotters (feet), about 225 g (8 oz) each, split half-way through from toes up

salt and freshly ground black pepper

any available fresh herbs, chopped

Mix the chicken stock, wine and sherry together, and bring to the boil. Sprinkle on the powdered gelatine and simmer for 10 minutes.

Melt the butter in a frying pan (skillet) and fry the onions gently until golden. Turn up the heat, add the chopped root vegetables, and cook for a few moments.

Transfer to a deep casserole dish and add the poussins, split trotters and seasoning to taste. Sprinkle with herbs and then pour on the hot liquid. Cover and place in a preheated oven at 180°C/350°F/mark 4 and cook for 1$\frac{1}{2}$ hours.

Turn off the oven and leave the dish to cool. Remove the dish from the oven and, when completely cold, put in the fridge to chill. The next day the poussins will be snugly encased in a lovely flavourful jelly.

Overleaf: for a boating lunch, serve Savoury Cheese Balls (opposite), Picnic Meat Pie (page 60), a mixed salad and Raspberry Syllabub Trifle (page 61) in individual glasses.

Boned Stuffed Quail

Quail are being farmed now in increasing numbers, and can be purchased boned which is by far the easiest way to handle and, more important still, to serve them. Fiddling about with unboned quail using a knife and fork is beyond me as I am a lazy eater. I want to get things into my mouth and down to my belly with the minimum of effort!

The birds can be stuffed the day before you want to cook them, and left wrapped in the kitchen foil in the fridge. They will come to no harm. If cooking on the barbecue, the cooking time depends very much on the heat of your charcoal and the distance between charcoal and cooking tray.

SERVES 6

6 boned quail

butter

STUFFING

350 g (12 oz) chicken breast, boned and skinned

45 ml (3 tablespoons) natural (plain) yoghurt

3 eggs

225 ml (7½ fl oz/¾ cup) double (heavy) cream

salt and freshly ground black pepper

12 black or green grapes, halved and seeded

Make the stuffing first. Cut the chicken breast into smallish pieces and marinate in the yoghurt for at least 24 hours. Put into your food processor and blend for a few seconds, dropping in the eggs one at a time. Stop the machine every now and again, and wipe down the sides to make sure all is mixed smoothly together. Take the bowl off the machine and keep in the fridge overnight or for 12 hours at least, when the mixture will go a shade darker and look decidedly gelatinous. Assemble the food processor once again and, with the machine operating at high speed, dribble in the cream *very slowly* to give you a dropping batter. Season well with salt and pepper.

Cut out six 15–17.5 cm (6–7 inch) squares of foil, place each square shiny side down on your work surface, and butter well the duller side facing you. Make one end of each quail tight and secure with two cocktail sticks, and spoon the chicken mixture into the other end. Press four halves of pipped grapes into each quail, and once again bring the skin over and hold in place firmly with two cocktail sticks. Bring up the four corners of the foil, fold over tightly, and your package is ready for either chilled storage, or for barbecue or oven. Over good hot coals, they will take about 30 minutes to cook through; in an oven preheated to 180°C/350°F/mark 4, they will need about 35 minutes.

Savoury Chicken Drumsticks in Yoghurt with Cornflakes

Eat hot if you like, but these are lovely cold for picnic fare.

6 chicken drumsticks
600 ml (1 pint/2½ cups) natural
  (plain) yoghurt
salt and freshly ground black
  pepper
at least 75 g (3 oz/3 cups)
  cornflakes, crushed

Simply marinate the chicken drumsticks in the seasoned natural (plain) yoghurt for 4 days, covered, in the fridge, turning them twice daily.

Take out of the marinade and coat with the crushed cornflakes. Turn and press so that the whole drumstick is completely covered. Place on a greased baking tray.

Place in a preheated oven at 190°C/375°F/mark 5 and bake for 30 minutes. Turn the heat up to 220°C/425°F/mark 7 and cook for a further 30 minutes after turning.

The same quantity of crushed crisps (potato chips) or savoury breadcrumbs (see page 24) may be used for the coating instead of the cornflakes.

Baked Trout in Coriander Butter

Three medium fresh trout, topped, tailed and gutted, will give you six fillets sufficient for a starter course – or else buy six trout and double the other ingredients, and you have a simple main course. If you're going to barbecue these, wrap the fillets (or the whole gutted fish) in foil, with half the coriander butter on top. Bake in the foil, and garnish when unwrapped with the orange slice and remaining butter (take in a freezer bag or box).

SERVES 6
6 trout fillets
175 g (6 oz/¾ cup) soft butter
45 ml (3 tablespoons) freshly
  ground coriander seeds, sieved
6 slices fresh orange
fresh parsley

Beat the soft butter and ground coriander together using an electric hand-held whisk. Arrange the trout fillets, skin side down, on a buttered baking tray, and spread with half the coriander butter. Cover with clingfilm (plastic wrap) and leave in the fridge until you need to cook.

Preheat oven to 180°C/350°F/mark 4, and the trout will take 15–20 minutes to cook. Meanwhile put the balance of the butter in a piping bag fitted with a star nozzle and pipe a twirl on each of the orange slices. Garnish with miniature pieces of fresh parsley. Serve on top of the cooked fish fillets.

Turnovers

These are an upmarket Cornish pasty really, and as they can be made and then frozen uncooked, it is only a matter of defrosting, baking, serving and eating thereafter! They're so handy for taking on picnics or walks.

If you find these are to your liking, you can adapt the fillings to your heart's content: any leftover cooked salmon can be mixed with a little chopped bulb fennel, hard-boiled egg and herbs; any leftover roast meat can be minced and flavoured with curry powder, chutney or mustard with an appropriate fruit.

MAKES 6 TURNOVERS
225 g ($\frac{1}{2}$ lb) puff pastry
filling of choice (see opposite)
1 egg, beaten with a pinch of salt
    and a grind of black pepper

To my mind, there is no doubt at all that home-made puff pastry is better, but you *can* use bought stuff. When the pastry is at room temperature, roll it out on a well floured surface gently and slowly until it is about 3 mm ($\frac{1}{8}$ inch) thick and a 32.5 × 47.5 cm (13 × 19 inch) rectangle. You don't have to use a ruler, but it does help as you then cut out six 15 cm (6 inch) squares. (Please, when rolling out puff pastry, don't act like a steamroller flattening tarmac on a road: you'll stretch and damage the pastry.)

Mix your filling ingredients together (see opposite).

Arrange the squares of pastry on your work surface, and paint the egg wash over the pastry surfaces facing you, using a small paintbrush. In your mind's eye, run a line on each square from the top left-hand corner down to the bottom right-hand corner: in the middle of the triangle on your left, place a portion of the filling, then bring the right-hand triangle over. Press the two edges gently together initially, and then use the back of a fork to impress deeply and securely in order to keep the filling inside during cooking. Paint with the remaining egg wash and either freeze or put in the fridge if you're going to bake them shortly afterwards.

Preheat the oven to 230°C/450°F/mark 8 and place the turnovers on baking sheets. Bake for 20 minutes until very brown and crisp (there is *nothing* worse than slightly soggy puff pastry).

Previous page: Turnovers (above) are ideal for rucksack picnics. Take along some fresh fruit such as cherries for afters and a thermos of 'Cowboy' Coffee (opposite).

Cheese, Chutney and Onion

225 g (8 oz/2 cups) coarsely grated Cheddar
   cheese
100 g (4 oz) onions, peeled and coarsely
   chopped
60 ml (4 tablespoons) chutney of choice

Chicken, Mushroom and Sweetcorn (Corn on the Cob)

300 g (10 oz) cooked chicken, flaked
100 g (4 oz/2 cups) mushrooms (or stalks)
50 g (2 oz/½ cup) sweetcorn (corn on the cob)
   kernels, cooked

Tongue and Cherry

350 g (12 oz) tongue, chopped coarsely
175 g (6 oz/1 cup) fresh unstoned cherries
   (if you stoned the cherries first, the cherries
   would go all squashy. Just warn your guests
   before they munch!)

Savoury Mince (Ground Beef or Lamb)

450 g (1 lb) savoury mince (ground beef or
   lamb) (see page 118)

'Cowboy' Coffee

Iced in summer or nice and warm in the winter, this is delicious. It can be made well ahead of time and simply stored cold or hot in a large thermos flask. If you have any teetotal guests the flavour of the nutmeg will mask the booze, and I bet you ten to one that they will be the first to return for seconds!

SERVES 6
1.2 litres (2 pints/5 cups) milk
90 ml (6 teaspoons) instant coffee
90 ml (6 teaspoons) soft brown
   sugar
1 whole nutmeg, finely grated
25 g (1 oz) milk, or plain (semi-
   sweet), chocolate, grated
90 ml (6 tablespoons) cooking
   brandy or rum

Try to use the best instant coffee available – I settle for Nestlé's Nescafé Gold Blend. Put all the ingredients except for the brandy into a saucepan and lightly whisk as it heats. When the milk comes to the boil and the chocolate has melted, add the cooking brandy or rum. Put into the thermos or leave to cool.

If you're serving it at home, hot from the pan, sprinkle on the merest suggestion of ground cinnamon. If serving cold, it is even better if – just prior to serving – you put it into your liquidizer with a portion of home-made ice cream and garnish with grated chocolate.

Overleaf: individual Pizzas (page 52) with a huge variety of toppings are ideal for many weekend entertaining occasions.

Individual Pizzas

If you have a dough hook on your mixer, pizzas are easy to make and just the thing to take on a walk for a snack lunch.

MAKES 6 PIZZA BASES

100 g (4 oz/¾ cup) strong plain
   (hard all purpose) flour, sieved
½ teaspoon salt
just under 15 g (½ oz) fresh yeast
   (1 cake compressed yeast)
2.5 ml (½ teaspoon) sugar
15 ml (1 tablespoon) warm milk
25 g (1 oz/2 tablespoons) butter,
   melted
1 egg yolk, beaten

Sieve the flour and salt into the mixer bowl. In another bowl, cream the yeast and sugar together, then add the warm milk, along with the melted butter and beaten egg yolk. Have the machine on the slowest speed to begin with and slowly dribble the liquid mixture into the mixer bowl. When all is combined with the dough hook, increase the speed and beat until you have a well blended, smooth dough. Remove from the bowl, place in a polythene bag, and leave in a warm place (the airing cupboard, on top of the stove, but definitely out of draughts) until it puffs up, almost doubling in size.

Meanwhile, make the topping (see below and opposite).

When the dough has risen, knock it back, divide into six balls, and roll flat. Arrange on greased baking sheets and bake for 10 minutes in an oven preheated to 190°C/375°F/mark 5. After the 10 minutes, remove from oven, arrange the topping ingredients over the bases, and return to the oven for a further 10 minutes.

TOPPINGS

Salami and Tomato Provençale

25 g (1 oz/2 tablespoons) butter
2 fat juicy garlic cloves, peeled
   and crushed with some salt
50 g (2 oz) onions, peeled and
   finely chopped
450 g (1 lb) tomatoes, skinned,
   seeded and roughly chopped
8 ml (½ tablespoon) tomato paste
450 ml (¾ pint/2 cups) double
   (heavy) cream, reduced by half
225 g (8 oz) salami of choice,
   skinned and very thinly sliced

Melt the butter and fry the garlic and onions until golden. Add the prepared tomatoes and tomato paste and leave to simmer until the sauce thickens, about 30 minutes. This makes 300 ml (½ pint/1¼ cups) of tomato provençale.

After the 10-minute baking of the pizza base, spread with layers of half the tomato provençale mixture and half the reduced cream. Fan the salami slices out on each pizza and top with the balance of the tomato and cream. Return to the oven to finish cooking.

Smoked Salmon, Waterchestnut and Fennel

450 ml ($\frac{3}{4}$ pint/2 cups) double
   (heavy) cream, reduced by half
225 g (8 oz) smoked salmon,
   cubed or thickly sliced
6 waterchestnuts, finely chopped
$\frac{1}{2}$ fennel bulb, finely chopped

*A*fter the 10-minute baking of the pizza base, remove from oven and spread with half the reduced cream. Arrange the other three ingredients on top, then cover with the balance of the cream. Return to the oven to finish cooking.

Savoury Lamb with Coriander

300 ml ($\frac{1}{2}$ pint/1$\frac{1}{4}$ cups) tomato
   provençale (see opposite)
225 g (8 oz) cooked lamb, minced
1 garlic clove, peeled and
   crushed
$\frac{1}{2}$ tablespoon coriander seeds,
   pounded to dust, then sieved
450 ml ($\frac{3}{4}$ pint/2 cups) double
   (heavy) cream, reduced by half

*M*ix the tomato sauce, lamb, garlic and coriander together. Spread half the cream over the pizza bases after their 10-minute baking, and top with the meat/tomato mixture, then the remaining cream. Return to the oven to finish cooking.

Pork with Sage, Onion and Apple Purée

225 g (8 oz/2 cups) green apples,
   peeled, cored and sliced
1 tablespoon sugar
50 g (2 oz/4 tablespoons) butter
100 g (4 oz) onions, peeled and
   finely chopped
225 g (8 oz) pork, minced
30 ml (2 tablespoons) chopped
   sage leaves
450 ml ($\frac{3}{4}$ pint/2 cups) double
   (heavy) cream, reduced by half

*P*ut the sliced apple in a pan with the sugar and cook gently until the apple falls into a purée. Melt the butter and cook the onion and pork until golden with the chopped sage. Liquidize the meat mixture, then mix with the apple purée. Spread half the reduced cream over the pizza bases after their 10-minute cooking, and top with the meat/apple mixture and the remaining cream. Return to the oven to continue cooking.

Cheese, Bacon and Olives

100 g (4 oz/1 cup) Cheddar
   cheese, grated
3 rashers smoked bacon, diced
12 black olives

*S*prinkle cheese on partly cooked pizzas and then arrange bacon strips in a trellis pattern with 2 olives on each pizza. Continue cooking.

Profiteroles

The mistake most people make when cooking choux pastry is that they tend to take it out of the oven far too soon, before it's cooked hard *enough. If really well cooked until they're what I call 'rock' hard (I'm sure you know what I mean), the profiteroles will freeze very well, and won't go sad and soggy when defrosted; they won't disintegrate when soggy fillings are inserted; and, best of all, they will last filled while you travel to picnic site or beach. Ideal travelling fodder in fact.*

If you serve them at home, two each will do for a main course, but note that the fillings are for six *only, not for the full 12 profiteroles that you can make from the pastry ingredients.*

MAKES 12 × 5 cm (2 inch)
PROFITEROLES
450 ml ($\frac{3}{4}$ pint/2 cups) water
175 g (6 oz/$\frac{3}{4}$ cup) butter, broken into pieces
225 g (8 oz/1$\frac{1}{2}$ cups) strong plain (hard all purpose) flour, well sieved
a pinch of salt
6 eggs, lightly beaten
FILLING
450 ml ($\frac{3}{4}$ pint/2 cups) double (heavy) cream
sea salt
additional ingredients of choice (see opposite)

Preheat the oven to 200°C/400°F/mark 6, and line some baking trays with dampened greaseproof (wax) paper. Have a piping bag with a plain nozzle at the ready too.

Put the water and butter into a saucepan and heat gently. DO NOT BOIL. When the butter has melted turn the heat up to high and add the flour and salt all at once. Beat vigorously with a wooden spoon to form a dough, about 1 minute. Take off the heat, cool slightly, and then start adding the eggs a little at a time. Never add more egg until the last addition has been taken up by the dough. The mixture will turn from a dull stodge to a shiny dropping batter consistency, and come away from the sides of the pan. Beat for a moment before putting in the piping bag.

Pipe the 12 profiteroles on to the dampened paper on the trays and place them in the oven, which you turn up immediately to 220°C/425°F/mark 7. Cook for 25–35 minutes until they are brown and very firm. Slit them at the sides and leave for a few minutes longer to allow steam to escape and the profiteroles to firm up as much as possible. Remove from the oven and leave to cool on a cooling tray.

I must admit that I am extravagant with the filling – as you can see! – as I only use *reduced* double (heavy) cream (why there's so much listed), and believe you me, there is nothing, but nothing like it. It is decidedly wicked, rich and bad for you – but, oh so tasty and good. It is simply used as a binding for the filling ingredients. Pour the cream into the largest (widthwise) saucepan you have and add a pinch of sea salt. Only place *half* the saucepan width over your hob as double cream has the horrible habit of suddenly, always when your back is turned, bubbling like a Vesuvius about to erupt, and then pouring all over your stove. If you only put half of the saucepan on the heat, the cream will automatically throw itself back into the non-heated side of the saucepan. But you should always keep your eye on the pan as the cream only takes about 10–15 minutes to reduce by half, changing in colour to the deepest cream, practically like a farm-made, summer butter pat.

This, when cool, is combined with one of the following fillings, which are then divided into six and put in the middle of the hard, ball-shaped profiteroles.

1. 400 g (14 oz) cooked flaked salmon mixed with very thin slices of radish and finely chopped chives.
2. 200 g (7 oz/2 cups) each cubed cooked chicken and ham, with a couple of teaspoons of Dijon mustard in the cream (or more if you like things hot). Add any fresh chopped herbs you may have in the garden.
3. 300 g (10 oz) sausagemeat (bulk sausage) cooked with 25 g (1 oz/2 tablespoons) butter and 100 g (4 oz/$\frac{3}{4}$ cup) finely chopped onions. Add some fresh sage with nuts of your choice folded in (pecans are particularly nice).
4. In summer, I like to fold 400 g (14 oz) smoked mackerel into the cream (make sure all the fine hair bones are removed first, please), and then I add whole dessert gooseberries.
5. There is no reason why you shouldn't resort to the savoury mince (ground beef or lamb) yet again (see page 118), but add some chopped salted peanuts to provide a pleasant change of texture – and paint the tops of the profiteroles with some Bovril (Miso) let down with a little water!

Wheatmeal Pastry Quiches

This 450 g (1 lb) mixing will give you sufficient pastry to make two 5 cm (2 inch) deep quiche bases of 22.5 cm (9 inch) in diameter. Use those lovely loose-bottomed, fluted flan tins (pans). Alternatively, the pastry could make two shallow 25 cm (10 inch) quiche bases or twelve individual bases of 10 cm (4 inch) in diameter — or, of course, a combination of the two (one large plus six small)! Freeze the pastry you don't use now for later.

Wheatmeal Pastry

225 g (8 oz) wheatmeal (brown) flour

225 g (8 oz/1½ cups) plain (all-purpose) flour

10 ml (2 teaspoons) curry powder

a pinch of salt

300 g (10 oz/1¼ cups) soft butter

2 eggs, lightly beaten

Make this wheatmeal pastry in the same way as the sweet pastry on page 78: mix the dry ingredients together on the work surface, plonk the butter in a well in the middle, and then pour the eggs on top; tip-tap away with your fingertips until of scrambled egg texture, then cut together to a dough with your palette knife. Divide into two balls and chill in polythene bags.

Bring out of the fridge and leave to come back to room temperature. Roll out and line the chosen quiche base. Leave to chill again.

When well chilled, cover with foil, fill with baking beans and bake blind in the oven preheated to 160°C/325°F/mark 3 – for 30 minutes for the large bases, or for 15–20 minutes for the small ones. Remove the foil and beans, and if necessary, return to the turned-off oven for another 5–10 minutes.

Quiche Custard

225 g (8 oz/1 cup) filling of choice (see opposite)

CUSTARD

300 ml (½ pint/1¼ cups) double (heavy) cream

2 eggs

1 egg yolk

salt and freshly ground black pepper

a pinch of freshly grated nutmeg

The following quantity of custard fills six individual quiche bases or one shallow 25 cm (10 inch) quiche base. To fill a deep 22.5 cm (9 inch) quiche base you will need *double* the custard quantity, and 300 g (10 oz/1¼ cups) filling of choice.

Simply beat the custard ingredients together and pour, in conjunction with one of the fillings below, into the quiche base or bases. In the oven preheated to 190°C/375°F/mark 5, bake the small quiches for 20 minutes, the shallow large quiches for about 35 minutes, and the deep one for about 45 minutes.

Quiche Fillings

You can use virtually any filling in the custard, and quiches are a good way of using up things you have left over in the fridge. I used some canned lobster mixed with canned red salmon in the deep quiche the other day, and everybody enjoyed it.

The filling can be a single veg – asparagus, broccoli, cauliflower, courgette (zucchini), fennel, leek, mushrooms or (bell) peppers, etc. – or a mixture, and you can always add extra suitable flavouring such as some grated cheese, chopped nuts, mustard, olives or pine kernels, etc. The vegetable ingredients must be of an even size – the courgettes in slices, peppers in strips and broccoli and cauli in florets – and if making the *smaller* quiches, the ingredients must be cut smaller in proportion.

The following combinations are some new ones I've tried:

1. Cauliflower florets, onion and red (bell) pepper marmalade (see page 153), and grated Cheddar cheese.
2. Sliced mushrooms, rinded and chopped bacon fried until crisp, and roughly crushed salted peanuts.
3. Broccoli florets, diced red pepper and thinly sliced courgettes. Use 90 ml (6 tablespoons) less cream in the custard and substitute with 90 ml (6 tablespoons) Marsala wine.
4. Defrosted frozen peas and sweetcorn (corn on the cob) kernels with finely diced cored fresh pineapple rings, topped with some toasted desiccated (shredded) coconut.
5. Flaked smoked haddock, thinly sliced hard-boiled eggs (arranged on pastry base), and some Keta (see page 20).

Overleaf: amidst autumn splendours, warm up with some Curried Leftover Vegetable Soups (page 101), then indulge in some Profiteroles (page 54), a slice of Boiled Loaf (page 69) and some fresh fruit.

Picnic Meat Pie

Don't faint when you see the amount of meat this pie needs – but it will give six very generous helpings and leave some over for snacks for the rest of the weekend. It's delicious served cold with home-made chutney or tomato provençale (see page 52), along with a huge bowl of salad and some thickly buttered bread – and it's easily transported in its tin for security, wrapped in a food bag.

1 × cheese pastry recipe (see
   page 141)
a good 1.5 kg (3½ lb) lean lamb,
   beef or pork, minced (ground)
25 g (1 oz/3 tablespoons) sea salt
15 g (½ oz/2 tablespoons) black
   peppercorns
6 eggs, beaten
flavourings of choice (see below)

Make the pastry, divide into balls as on page 141, and leave to chill. When it is brought back to room temperature, roll out the larger ball and use to line a loose-bottomed 22.5 cm (9 inch) flan tin which is about 5 cm (2 inch) deep. Leave to chill. Line with foil, fill with baking beans and bake blind at 160°C/325°F/ mark 3 for 30–40 minutes.

Meanwhile mix the minced (ground) meat with the sea salt and black peppercorns which have been ground to a powder in your mortar and pestle. Fold the eggs into the seasoned meat. If you like, enhance the beef with a tablespoon of dry English mustard powder; the pork with 4 dried sage leaves, finely crumbled; and the lamb with a generous sprinkling of freshly ground coriander. Or take out 225–350 g (8–12 oz) of the meat and substitute with roughly chopped hazelnuts, walnuts or cooked chestnuts.

Press the meat down into the cooked, cold base. Make a lid with the rest of the pastry, cover the whole pie with a double thickness of foil, and bake in the preheated oven at 190°C/375°F/mark 5 for 45 minutes. Remove the foil, and cook for a further 45 minutes. Take out and leave to go cold.

Vegetable Kebabs

These can be prepared ahead of time, and are good for an impromptu meal as they are easily reheated. In fact ideal for a situation when guests arrive in dribs and drabs and want to eat on arrival. They are also good to take on a barbecue picnic as they are done in minutes over hot coals, and look *so good.*

You need kebab skewers obviously (without wooden ends if they are to go in the oven) and, to serve six, 150 g (5 oz/1 cup) each of parsnips, carrots, turnip or swede (rutabaga), courgettes (zucchini) and leek.

Cut the root vegetables into even sizes of about 2 cm ($\frac{3}{4}$ inch) square, and blanch in boiling salted water for 8 minutes. The courgettes, which you will have attractively scored and cut into 2 cm ($\frac{3}{4}$ inch) slices, will need only 4 minutes' blanching, as will the leek rounds.

Sit down quietly for a few minutes and thread them all on to your skewers. If you're cooking them at home, lay the skewers over a baking pan, both ends of the skewers resting on the rim of the pan. Paint liberally with melted (perhaps flavoured) butter or walnut oil, season well, and heat through for 15 minutes in the preheated oven at 190°C/375°F/mark 5. Or, simply lay the buttered or oiled and seasoned skewers on the barbecue grid for a few minutes, turning frequently. Serve as a generous vegetable accompaniment, or as a vegetarian main course with some mashed potatoes or rice.

Apart from the basic root vegetables, more upmarket veg may be used: thin aubergine (eggplant) diamonds (left to one side with salt for a couple of hours to extract the bitter juices), red, green or yellow (bell) pepper diamonds, mushroom caps, onion pieces, cherry tomatoes, baby sweetcorn (corn on the cob) and even large radishes. These do not need pre-cooking.

Raspberry Syllabub Trifle

This dish can, of course, be prepared in a conventional see-through trifle dish, but it looks stunning if served in individual tall champagne or knickerbocker glory glasses.

Simply build up layers of sponge cake (see page 72) topped with a generous measure of a sweet dessert wine or sherry, and a spoonful of custard. I make a rich one with 8 eggs, 50 g/2 oz/3 tablespoons caster (super fine) sugar and 600 ml/1 pint/2$\frac{1}{2}$ cups single (light) cream. Top this with a spoonful of raspberry purée (see page 124) and carry on the layers until the glasses are filled. A generous dollop of the syllabub (see page 139) is the crowning glory with a mint leaf to add a bit of colour. I also like one of those chocolate flakes crushed on the top.

The syllabub could be one of the layers as well, with the raspberry purée as the topping. Don't forget to use long-handled spoons, otherwise guests will dig in vain!

Overleaf: on the barbecue, foil-baked Boned Stuffed Quail (page 44) and Trout in Coriander Butter (page 45), and served with barbecued Vegetable Kebabs (opposite).

AFTERNOON TEAS

The partaking of afternoon tea seems to be declining, and I put it all down to this awful desire for skeletal thinness that everyone seems to have acquired. I suppose, too, that with the speed of life today, many of us don't have the actual time to stop and sit down for an hour, a nibble and a chat at four o'clock in the afternoon. But it's a *wonderful* institution, so quintessentially British, and I serve it enthusiastically whenever I can. It's a marvellous way of welcoming guests who arrive mid afternoon, thirsty and hungry after negotiating the motorway and side roads, and nothing could be better after a lengthy post-lunch walk, than to come in to a good cuppa and something delicious to eat. It's especially welcome in the winter when we seem to need more to keep us going: light the fire, draw the curtains, make some hot toast and tuck in!

I pull out all the stops, using beautiful tablecloths and napkins, often Victorian ones found on market stalls or specialist shops, and my prettiest china. I recently bought a delightfully patterned tea service in the finest bone china which was for six but was minus two cups, had one badly chipped saucer, and a cracked plate. The cream jug and sugar basin were fine though, and so I have enough of this set for *four*. I think I must have four similar services at the farm now, but I still can't resist them. Naturally I do have a proper one (Wedgwood) to match the dinner service, and this is used on high days and holidays (or when the bank manager or solicitor and their wives visit).

You will also be amazed at how inexpensive pastry knives and forks can be in junk shops. All they need often is the ivory cleaned with lemon juice and a polish of the silver, and look lovely on the plates. Old glass cake stands can be bought for £2 or £3, and I am on the look-out for one of those wooden three- or four-tier folding cake stands which my Nan used to bring out when Auntie Janie came for tea. Keep your eyes open, too, for those old-fashioned crocheted milk jug covers edged with fancy beads, and you can still find those large mosquito netting covers from Colonial days that have been lovingly sewn with fancy beads to weigh the sides down and cover a tea tray completely. Good paper napkins can be bought and then disposed of, but for me once again those lovely real linen Victorian ones cannot be beaten.

Afternoon tea can be formal or informal but with all the crumbs that invariably go with this meal it is much better if you sit up at the table, whether inside or outside in the garden in the summer. At least you won't be quite so tired at the end of the afternoon, having endlessly gone round offering plates of this and that. In my eyes there is nothing quite so good as a groaning table piled high with goodies, but if when your table is laid, you find there are gaps, there is no reason whatsoever why you shouldn't put some *objets d'art* about.

As for the food itself, for a proper afternoon tea – as enshrined in tradition – you should always start with sandwiches. These should be thin, crustless, dainty and elegant – or try my mini twirls. Thereafter you should go on to scones or buttered loaf or tea cakes, to be followed by the sweet iced or creamed cakes, tarts and biscuits. In actuality, though, this is often too much, but it depends on what your food plans are for the rest of the day, and on what you have already eaten. A *huge* afternoon tea would be welcome after a lunch-less drive, but it might spoil guests' appetites for dinner; if you go for a walk *after* tea, or play tennis, however, appetites can be built up again! And if you've carried a picnic tea on a trek across the fells, something substantial plus a good swig of iced lemonade, tea or coffee from a thermos would be much appreciated.

The individual recipes, once again, are ones which, on the whole, can have been made in advance. Some can be frozen, some can be kept successfully for a few days in an airtight container, and only a few, like the sandwiches and the tartlet filling, need last-minute action.

As for the tea itself, choose something delicious from the huge array available these days. Try to have at least two kinds on offer: I love more esoteric types like mango, passionfruit or blackcurrant, but often guests might prefer Earl Grey or a strong Indian. Remember, too, to have a few thin slices of scored lemon available as more and more people are drinking weak tea with lemon. Make sure you have at least two electric kettles on the go and make *fresh* pots of tea after 10 minutes because the tea will begin to go bitter. Use a slop bowl on the table to pour out the dregs before starting the tea ritual all over again. And, yes, I hope you are an MIF person – milk in first!

Mini Twirl Sandwiches

I invariably use bought sliced thin bread for making my sandwiches. One slice will give you 12 mini twirls when you have removed the crusts (save for savoury breadcrumbs, see page 24). Each slice is rolled much thinner with a heavy wooden rolling pin, then spread with leftover hollandaise (see page 138), soft butter or butter flavoured with vinegar, ground hazelnuts or the juice and rind of a lemon or orange – just to give that hint of something slightly different in the sandwich.

For six slices of bread you will need 50 g (2 oz/4 tablespoons) butter to spread. Thereafter, you will need one of the following fillings.

1. *4 hard-boiled eggs, very finely chopped, mixed with 30 ml (2 tablespoons) cream and the heads of a small carton of mustard and cress.*
2. *100 g (4 oz/½ cup) cheese and herb pâté (see page 148).*
3. *1 × 175 g (6 oz) can tongue, liquidized with 10 ml (2 teaspoons) prepared mustard and a generous sprig of fresh parsley.*
4. *1 × 175 g (6 oz) can tuna in oil, liquidized with 1 small bunch of white spring onions (scallions) and 15 ml (1 tablespoon) tomato purée (paste).*
5. *1 × 175 g (6 oz) can salmon, liquidized with 15 ml (1 tablespoon) home-made mayonnaise and 6 sprigs of fresh dill.*
6. *1 × 175 g (6 oz) can sardines liquidized with 30 ml (2 tablespoons) cooked peas and a generous touch of Worcestershire sauce.*

When spread, roll the slice up like a sausage, filling inside (obviously), and slice thinly into 12 mini-twirls. If you are going to prepare the sandwiches in the morning, leave them rolled up like sausages, unsliced, and covered with the damp outer leaves of lettuce (the ones you would discard) or a damp teatowel. Always slice into twirls as late as possible.

I think individual plates for each guest are much better as they can be attractively garnished with sprigs of parsley, cucumber twirls, cherry tomatoes or radish flowers. Also, this way you simply hand out the plates once, and you're not continually bobbing up and down tempting people to take another. This brings out the worst in me as invariably the guests want another but feel it polite to decline, and then you have to go through all the rigmarole of "Oh, go on, they are so small", then "Well, if you insist, I will just take one" . . . !

Previous page: for a summer afternoon tea, serve Mini-Twirl Sandwiches (above), Sweet Pastry Tartlets (page 78), Orange Wedge Cake and Iced Tea (both page 76).

Mini Wheatmeal Loaves

A necessity is those tiny little loaf pans. You could also make larger loaves, in two well greased 450 g (1 lb) loaf pans, which should be baked for about 40 minutes.

MAKES 12 TINY LOAVES

225 g (8 oz/1½ cups) wheatmeal (brown) flour

225 g (8 oz/1½ cups) strong plain (hard all-purpose) flour

10 ml (2 teaspoons) salt

75 g (3 oz/6 tablespoons) soft butter

25 g (1 oz) fresh yeast (1 cake compressed yeast)

10 ml (2 teaspoons) caster (superfine) sugar

250 ml (8 fl oz/1 cup) lukewarm water

Put the sifted flours and salt, plus the butter, into your mixer bowl and, using the dough hook, mix.

Meanwhile cream the yeast and sugar together, then add the lukewarm water. Mix, then pour into the flour mixture, and slowly beat until a dough forms.

Remove the dough from the machine, put in a bowl, and cover with a teatowel. Leave somewhere nice and warm, completely free from draughts, to double in size (the timing will depend on the warmth of the place).

Lightly punch the mixture back down and divide into 12 equal portions. Roll each one gently into a ball and then lightly press into the greased pans. Cover with the teatowel again and return to your cossetting venue. When doubled in size once again, bake in the preheated oven at 220°C/425°F/mark 7 for 20 minutes. Leave in the pan for a few minutes, then turn on to a cooling tray to become cold.

Boiled Loaf

A fruit loaf to be served in slices, well buttered, which you could also make in 2 × 450 g (1 lb) loaf tins. Use a standard cup which holds 250 ml (8 fl oz).

MAKES 1 × 900 g (2 lb) LOAF

1 cup cold water

1 cup sultanas (white raisins)

1 cup caster (superfine) sugar

100 g (4 oz/½ cup) butter

8 ml (1 heaped teaspoon) bicarbonate of soda (baking soda)

1 egg, lightly beaten

2 cups self-raising (self-rising) flour, sifted

Put the water, sultanas, sugar and butter in a deep saucepan, bring to the boil, and allow to simmer for 10 minutes. Remove from the heat and beat in the bicarbonate of soda (baking soda). Beware, as this often bubbles up to the top of the saucepan.

Leave to cool, and meanwhile grease, flour and sugar the tin (pan) or tins.

When the mixture is cool, beat in the egg and stir in the flour. Place in the oven preheated to 160°C/325°F/ mark 3 and bake for 1¼ hours to 1 hour 20 minutes. Turn out, cool, and store in an airtight container.

Sponges and Fairy (Cup) Cakes

This mixing will give you eight thin eight-portion sponge cakes, or six plus a dozen fairy cakes (see below). Use leftovers in trifle.

450 g (1 lb/2 cups) soft butter
450 g (1 lb/1¾ cups) caster (superfine) sugar
450 g (1 lb) eggs (normally 8 × No. 2/large out of their shells)
450 g (1 lb/3 cups) self-raising (self-rising) flour

The soft butter is placed in a large round-bottomed mixing bowl to which the sugar is added. Use your hands to combine these to a fairly creamy consistency. Then, using an electric hand-held whisk, beat for at least 8 minutes until light, white and fluffy.

In a separate bowl lightly beat the eggs together and then, *little by little*, add them, beating them into the mixture, *never* adding more until what you have originally added has worked itself through the mixing. Remove three-quarters of this mix and divide between three other bowls, for four different flavours.

To the first one, add 60 ml (4 tablespoons) drinking chocolate (sweetened instant cocoa) made up to a good 100 g (4 oz/1 cup) with sieved self-raising flour.

To the second add 60 ml (4 tablespoons) desiccated (shredded) coconut and 60 ml (4 tablespoons) sultanas (white raisins) made up to a good 100 g (4 oz/1 cup) with sieved self-raising flour.

To the third add 60 ml (4 tablespoons) crushed dried banana flakes with 30 ml (2 tablespoons) each finely chopped preserved ginger and chopped walnuts. Make⁴ up once again to a good 100 g (4 oz/1 cup) with sieved self-raising flour.

The fourth one needs only have some vanilla essence (extract) and the 100 g (4 oz/¾ cup) self-raising flour. Or use 30 ml (2 tablespoons) Camp coffee (extra strong liquid coffee) instead of the vanilla essence.

You need a few 17.5 cm (7 inch) flat round cake tins (pans), and these should be greased, floured and sugared. Each of the above four mixings can be divided between two (in which case you need *eight* cake tins altogether), or make six cakes in six cake tins, and the remaining mixing will give you 12 fairy (cup) cakes portioned into paper cases in cup-cake baking tins.

Preheat the oven to 180°C/350°F/mark 4, and the

Previous page: a simple fireside tea of buttered toast with jam- and cream-filled Sponge Cake (above).

little fairy cakes take about 20 minutes, the large ones 20–30. When they are firm, remove them from the oven and leave for 10 minutes. Thereafter, turn them on to cooling trays.

When you want to serve, sandwich the larger cakes together with a flavoured cream (300 ml/½ pint/1¼ cups will do one double cake) or a flavoured butter cream (225 g/8 oz/1 cup butter, 2 tablespoons Camp coffee and 175 g/6 oz/1½ cups icing (confectioners') sugar is nice). Lemon curd is a good filling too (see page 154). Thereafter, all you need to do is sieve icing (confectioners') sugar over, pipe twirls of fresh whipped cream on top, and decorate with fruit or mint leaves. Fill the fairy cakes with the same, or simply ice.

Apple and Date Batter Ginger Slice

Simplicity itself to make and a joy to eat but I must admit I am piggish and am overgenerous with butter on the slices!

MAKES 2 × 450 g (1 lb) CAKES
175 g (6 oz/1¼ cups) self-raising (self-rising) flour
2.5 ml (½ teaspoon) mixed spice
50 g (2 oz/3 tablespoons) demerara (brown) sugar
10 ml (2 teaspoons) ground ginger
50 g (2 oz/4 tablespoons) butter
30 ml (2 tablespoons) treacle
2 eggs
150 ml (¼ pint/⅔ cup) milk
1 teaspoon bicarbonate of soda (baking soda)
100 g (4 oz/¾ cup) stoned dates, finely chopped
1 apple, peeled and cored

*P*lace all the ingredients with the exception of the milk, bicarb, dates and apple, into the food processor and combine. Bring the milk to the boil, then pour in, along with the bicarbonate of soda. Continue blending until nice and bubbly.

Remove from the processor, and divide between two greased and floured 450 g (1 lb) loaf tins (pans). Sprinkle the chopped dates over the contents of the pans, and then layer the thinly sliced apples on top. Bake in the preheated oven at 180°C/350°F/mark 4 for 1 hour. Serve, when cool, in slices.

Overleaf: when you've been expending energy, you need a hearty afternoon tea: serve bread and butter, slices of Apple and Date Batter Ginger Slice (above), and varied Fairy (Cup) Cakes (opposite).

Orange Wedge Cake

The addition of cornflour (corn starch) makes a particularly good textured cake.

6 eggs, separated

175 g (6 oz/$\frac{3}{4}$ cup) caster
  (superfine) sugar

juice and finely grated rind of 2
  oranges

75 g (3 oz/$\frac{1}{2}$ cup) plain (all-
  purpose) flour, sieved with 25 g
  (1 oz/scant $\frac{1}{4}$ cup) cornflour
  (corn starch) and a pinch of salt

FILLING/TOPPING

2 eggs

100 g (4 oz/$\frac{1}{2}$ cup) caster
  (superfine) sugar

juice and finely grated rind of 2
  oranges

300 ml ($\frac{1}{2}$ pint/1$\frac{1}{4}$ cups) double
  (heavy) cream

Line a deep 25 cm (10 inch) loose-bottomed cake tin (pan) with good greaseproof (wax) paper.

To make the cake, warm the mixing bowl and wire beaters, and place the six cake egg yolks in. Beat away for at least 6 minutes until the yolks are quite fluffy, then add the caster (superfine) sugar, a tablespoon at a time. Meanwhile warm the orange juice and rind and when all the sugar has been added, slowly dribble this into the mixture. Turn out into a large mixing bowl.

Wash the bowl and beaters and dry well (making sure no grease remains). Beat the egg whites until stiff.

Gently fold the sieved flour mixture into the yolk mixture and then fold in two-thirds of the stiffly beaten egg whites. Put the remaining third of the egg white back on the machine and continue beating. Fold in this balance. Turn the whole lot into the prepared pan and bake in the preheated oven at 180°C/350°F/mark 4 for 45 minutes.

Meanwhile make the filling/topping. Beat the eggs, sugar and orange rind and juice together, then put in a bowl over a pan of simmering water. Cook for 10–15 minutes, stirring from time to time, until it thickens. Leave to go cold and then pass through a fine plastic sieve into the cream. Whip up until thick.

Remove the cake from the tin and leave to go cold. Slice it in three horizontally and fill and coat with the creamy orange mixture.

Iced Tea

I know many people make this by simply pouring any leftover tea from the endless pots made during the day into a container and then leaving it to cool in the fridge. Worse still, many buy powdered tea which is supposed to be ideal for making this commodity!

I have to admit that I make an MGM production number of iced tea when entertaining during the summer. First of all I use cut-glass, half-pint mugs, Pimms cups, or those large fine scotch and soda glasses which are always polished to a high degree of sparkle! Placed on your best silver salver, these will add a touch of class to the occasion. I go out and collect fresh rose petals in abundance and place these in the base (about eight petals in each glass), along with a large sprig of fresh mint. Any leftover petals look lovely scattered between the glasses on the tray. In the days beforehand, I make lots of ice, filling up the ice-cube trays then emptying them when frozen into freezer bags.

Shortly before the guests arrive I put three ice cubes in each glass with a — wait for it — Earl Grey teabag, making sure the string and paper label are lying over the edge. As the guests step in, I simply pour boiling water into each glass. The guests can then dunk their own teabags until they get the strength of tea they like. I always put 2.5 ml ($\frac{1}{2}$ teaspoon) sugar in each glass as I think unsweetened iced tea can be rather bitter.

Pecan, Pineapple, Ginger and Hazelnut Frangipane

This can either be served as a cake at teatime, or as a dessert. If you have come across the exotic hazelnut liqueur, Frangelico, a sherry glass of this served chilled goes wonderfully!

1 × 20 cm (8 inch) pastry case (see page 78), baked blind

FILLING

100 g (4 oz/$\frac{1}{2}$ cup) butter

100 g (4 oz/$\frac{1}{2}$ cup) sugar

2 eggs, lightly beaten

75 g (3 oz/$\frac{1}{2}$ cup) self-raising (self-rising) flour, sieved

25 g (1 oz/$\frac{1}{4}$ cup) ground hazelnuts, sieved

$\frac{1}{4}$ fresh pineapple, skinned, cored and finely chopped

100 g (4 oz/1 cup) pecan nuts, finely chopped

1 whole round preserved (candied) ginger, finely chopped

To make the filling, cream the butter and sugar together in a bowl, and then beat in the eggs, a little at a time. Gently fold in the flour mixed with the hazelnuts, and then add the chopped pineapple, pecan nuts and ginger. Transfer to the blind-baked pastry case and bake in the preheated oven at 180°C/350°F/mark 4 for 45–55 minutes. Pierce with a fine skewer – it should come out clean – to double-check before removing from oven, then leave to go cold.

It can be iced or simply coated with sieved icing (confectioners') sugar and decorated with blobs and twirls of whipped flavoured double (heavy) cream.

Sweet Pastry Tartlets

This sweet pastry can be made well in advance and frozen. Always remember to bring it back to room temperature before working with it. You need to make the pastry the day before anyway, so that it has at least a night's thorough chilling.

This quantity of pastry will make 18 individual 10 cm (4 inch) flans or tartlets, but it could also make three 20–25 cm (8–10 inch) flan or tart (pie) bases, ideal for the frangipane in the previous recipe, for instance.

The sweetened cream cheese filling — use as much or as little as you like — is delicious with the summer fruit, but you could use a sweetened or flavoured whipped double (heavy) cream instead — or indeed lemon curd (see page 154).

450 g (1 lb/3 cups) plain (all-purpose) flour less 90 ml (6 tablespoons)
90 ml (6 tablespoons) icing (confectioners') sugar
300 g (10 oz/1¼ cups) soft butter
2 eggs
FILLING
good full-fat cream cheese
caster (superfine) sugar
fresh summer berries

Sieve the flour and icing (confectioners') sugar on to your work surface and make a well in the centre, into which you place the soft butter. Make indentations on the top of the butter with your fingertips so that the egg yolks will stay on top rather than run off when you break them on, as you now do.

Using your fingertips again, tip-tap away until the eggs are combined with the butter – it'll look rather like messy scrambled eggs – then get a large palette knife and flick the flour over this mixture. Taking the palette knife in both hands, smartly and sharply slice through the mixture at an angle of 90 degrees. Eventually small balls will form and quite quickly the pastry will come together. Divide into three balls (don't *squeeze* them), and leave overnight in the fridge in a polythene bag.

It is absolutely *essential* that you remove one or more balls a few hours before you wish to roll as the pastry *must* be as soft as it was when you had finished making it the day before.

Have ready some loose-bottomed, fluted 10 cm (4 inch) flan tins (pans) and cut each ball of pastry into six equal sections. Put the base of the first small flan tin on your work surface and sprinkle flour *around the edge*. Put the ball of pastry in the middle of the base and then, with your wooden rolling pin, gently roll the pastry away from the middle over on to the flour. This outer rim is then flipped back over the base with a palette knife, the base lifted up with the knife, and eased into the outer fluted rim. The pastry rims then fall into place. Line with kitchen foil and make sure it is taken right over the edges (to avoid blackened pastry edges). Leave to chill and set in the fridge. Repeat with the other pieces of pastry in the other flan tins.

When you wish to bake the flans blind, fill with lentils or split peas – or better still, those ceramic baking beans you can buy in upmarket kitchen shops – and preheat the oven to 160°C/325°F/mark 3. Bake blind for 30 minutes. Remove the beans and foil, make sure that the pastry shows no sign of fat (if it does, keep in until baked crisp), then leave to cool.

To make the filling, mix the cream cheese with sugar to taste, and pipe this over the base of each tartlet. Then arrange your sliced strawberries, whole raspberries, red or blackcurrants or gooseberries in a band across the top. Decorate if you like with whipped sweetened cream using a star-nozzled piping bag, and mint leaves.

Summer fruit tartlets can also be glazed by gently melting 60 ml (4 tablespoons) redcurrant jelly in a small saucepan with 15 ml (1 tablespoon) wine (or water). Spoon over your laid-out fruit.

Shortbread Rounds

These are super served simply with a cup of tea or with a lovely creamy pud, or they can be jammed together in pairs and then topped with coloured icing. They are even better if, along with the jam, you add a little flavoured butter cream!

The dough can be stored in the fridge if you only decide to cook half of it initially – or make this other half into tartlets as in the next recipe.

MAKES 20–24 ROUNDS

200 g (7 oz/⅔ cup) soft butter

75 g (3 oz/½ cup) caster (superfine) sugar

150 g (5 oz/1 cup) plain (all-purpose) flour, sifted

150 g (5 oz/1 cup) self-raising (self-rising) flour, sifted

a pinch of salt

Put all the ingredients into the mixer bowl and, using the beater, slowly combine to a dough.

Roll out on a lightly floured and caster-sugared work surface to 6 mm (¼ inch) thickness. Using a 6.25 cm (2½ inch) biscuit cutter or a strong inexpensive glass, cut out 20–24 circles. Place on a baking sheet lined with good greaseproof (wax) paper and bake in the preheated oven at 150°C/300°F/mark 2 for 30 minutes. Remove from the oven and, as they are cooling, sprinkle with vanilla sugar. When cold store in an airtight container. They'll keep for two weeks.

Shortbread Chocolate Marshmallow Tartlets

These are relatively easy to make if you buy in a packet of those lovely large round marshmallows. But do try making the marshmallows yourself as below!

Both shortbread and marshmallow recipes will make more than the six tartlets you might need – but I'm sure you'll find a good use for the leftover mixtures! The marshmallow, for instance, can be rolled into balls and then rolled in icing sugar or desiccated (shredded) coconut and eaten as a sweet or petit four.

1 × shortbread recipe (*see previous recipe*)

about 50 g (2 oz/⅓ cup) good chocolate

a little butter

5 ml (1 teaspoon) rum or brandy

toasted desiccated (shredded) coconut

MARSHMALLOW

150 ml (¼ pint/⅔ cup) cold water

15 g (½ oz/2 packets) powdered gelatine

225 g (8 oz/1 cup) caster (superfine) sugar

Combine the shortbread ingredients as in the previous recipe, but place large balls in individual small round tins (pans) and press firmly down and then up and around the edges to make a 'cup'. Leave to chill and then put an appropriately sized sponge cake paper case in each and fill with dried peas or beans. Bake in the preheated oven at 180°C/350°F/mark 4 for 30–40 minutes. Take the dried peas and paper cases out and return tins to the oven for 5–8 more minutes to dry out and finish cooking. Remove and leave to become cold.

Melt the chocolate in a pudding basin over a pan of simmering water, add the merest blob of butter and the rum or brandy, and when nice and smooth spoon into the cooked and cooled shortbread cases, making sure the chocolate goes right up the sides. It will set quickly into a very firm (but delicate) container.

To make the marshmallow, set a pudding basin over a saucepan of simmering water and put in half the water. Sprinkle on the gelatine and leave to melt until the liquid is clear. Put the sugar with the rest of the water in another saucepan and gently heat to melt the sugar. Bring to the boil and then boil until the temperature reaches 103°C/217°F, about 10 minutes. Transfer the clear gelatine liquid to a warmed Kenwood bowl, then pour on the boiled sugar and leave the machine to beat it at top speed for 10 minutes.

When you wish to serve, fill each chocolate shortbread case with home-made marshmallow (or cut some bought marshmallows to fit). Scatter some toasted desiccated coconut on top and you could flash them under the grill (broiler) just prior to serving. Or you could sear the tops decoratively with a skewer heated until red-hot over a flame.

Wheatmeal Scones

These are delicious served warm, split and spread thickly with butter and a good home-made jam or lemon curd (see page 154).

225 g (8 oz/1½ cups) self-raising
  (self-rising) flour
225 g (8 oz/1½ cups) wheatmeal
  (brown) flour
a pinch of salt
175 g (6 oz/¾ cup) soft butter
45 ml (3 tablespoons) caster
  (superfine) sugar
sultanas (white raisins) to taste
2 eggs, lightly beaten
sour cream, top of the milk or
  natural (plain) yoghurt to bind

Preheat the oven to 220°C/425°F/mark 7.
  Sieve the self-raising flour (self-rising) into a large bowl and add the wheatmeal (brown) flour and salt. Gently rub in the butter until you have fine crumbs and then add the caster (superfine) sugar and sultanas (white raisins). Mix well. Scatter the lightly beaten eggs over this mixture and ever so gently mix in. You will get the right action if you first of all hold your arm out and wobble it; wobble thus in the mix!

  Now it will depend on how warm your hands are, how large the eggs are, and how creamy the butter is as to how much binding 'liquid' you will need. But *don't* fall into the trap of putting too much in too soon, otherwise you will end up with a batter, not a scone mix. It should just hold. Turn out of the bowl on to a floured work surface and gently press into a rectangular shape about 2.5 cm (1 inch) thick. Use a palette knife to cut through the mix as economically as possible into diamond-shaped scones. Transfer to a baking sheet, and cook for 10–15 minutes.

  When cold, store in plastic bags for 2 days. To prepare them in advance, freeze the dough, *uncooked.*

Home-made Lemonade

Place the rind and juice of 6 lemons and 2 oranges into a large porcelain or earthenware jug (pitcher) and add 225 g (8 oz/1 cup) caster (superfine) sugar. Pour on 600 ml (1 pint) boiling water and stir occasionally. When cold, chill.

  Serve in gin and tonic glasses, garnished with scored slices of lemon and a large sprig of fresh mint (and the odd rose petal too if you like). It is very thirst-quenching and infinitely superior to most brands of bought lemonade.

Overleaf: for a tea beside the lake, choose Shortbread Chocolate Marshmallow Tartlets (opposite), Pecan, Pineapple, Ginger and Hazelnut Frangipane (page 77), and Lemonade (above).

High Teas

High tea is another part of the British culinary scene that seems to be fast disappearing, and it is such a pity. Very much a northern tradition – common in Scotland too, apparently – it's so useful at a weekend. If your guests have to leave before dinner, you could serve them a high tea at about 5 pm – the usual high tea hour – and that will keep them going happily throughout the evening's travels. A high tea is also a magnificent way in which to welcome *arriving* guests on a Friday, say, and it allows time for a walk, some sport or other form of socializing before a late supper if you felt like it. After all, everyone can go to bed late, as nobody has to get up the next morning for work! However, high tea isn't dainty like afternoon tea, it's a substantial meal, and the day's eating should be planned to fit in with that. A hearty Sunday lunch followed by a high tea would perhaps be a bit much; a good late brunch would be the ideal precursor of an earlyish high tea.

In my youth, we had high teas on the weekdays that we visited relatives after school had finished at four, and what spreads we used to encounter: sandwiches, hot toasted teacakes, scrambled or poached eggs (see pages 17 and 20), simple fish dishes (the smoked haddock chowder is typical), pies, cold meats and salads, chunks of good cheese, warm home-made bread, rib-sticking cakes, trifle (see page 61) and, occasionally, some fresh fruit and cream. And everything washed down with good strong tea. But everything had to be finished and definitely over before the men came home from the shipyard around six. Then we kids would retire to the parlour to be quiet, and I remember playing with the floor-standing HMV gramophone. I didn't play records, however, but used to open up the lid, wind the machine up, and then put objects on the turntable. I wanted to see how long before, and at what speed, they would be flung off when the turntable started to spin. It was well worth a clout on the ear if I were caught!

There are quite a few ideas in this section, but do look at the other sections too for recipes suitable for high teas. The basics are a combination of simple and savoury with the more substantial sweet cakes – no elegant tartlets at *this* meal! Everything is spread on the table for people to help themselves, and there is no real starter to main course progression, although the sweet things are eaten last, of course. Quiches and flans are a good basic, especially as the bases can be made in advance and frozen uncooked. I often use these bases as a container for the weekend leftovers on a Sunday, which means I can leave the farm with an empty fridge; some combinations have been wonderful, some less successful! See page 56 for how to make a wonderful wheatmeal (brown) pastry which can be made into varying sized quiches: small ones would be extra special on a high-tea table. There's a cheese pastry too, on page 141.

Another idea for pre-preparing during the week: if you are doing a roast, buy a larger one than you need, and the leftover meat will give you a start to your weekend stock of goodies. When the meat is cold, slice it very thinly. Arrange a large square of clingfilm (plastic wrap) on your work surface, and lightly paint it with a French dressing of choice (see page 93 for one idea). Pile up the slices on the clingfilm touching each one with a brush-stroke of the dressing. Wrap well in the clingfilm and then securely encase in foil. This will keep well in the fridge, and is extremely handy for sandwiches for peckish visitors, and can even be served with a plate of salad at a high tea.

Salads, too, play a major part at any high tea, and can also, of course, be served at any other meal throughout the day. I think I've given you enough ideas here! Chutneys are *vital*, and you'll find them in the Edible Gifts section.

Smoked Haddock Chowder with Baked Egg

Such a simple dish but one which gives me much pleasure each time I make it. Maybe it reminds me of my childhood days but it is a sluttish dish when wishing to be indulged!

SERVES 6

675 g (1½ lb) smoked haddock,
  boned and flaked
450 ml (¾ pint/2 cups) cold milk
100 g (4 oz) onions, peeled and
  finely chopped
75 g (3 oz/⅓ cup) butter
6 eggs

Divide the flaked smoked haddock between six dishes roughly 12.5–15 cm (5–6 inch) in diameter (I use Apilco), and put 75 ml (⅛ pint/¼ cup) milk in each. Divide the chopped onion between the dishes, then put 15 g (½ oz/1 tablespoon) butter on top of each.

Put the dishes in a roasting tin (pan) and fill it with enough boiling water to come half-way up the sides of the dishes. Cover the whole thing with kitchen foil and cook in the preheated oven at 180°C/350°F/mark 4 for 20 minutes.

Remove the foil, break in the eggs – one per dish – and return the tray to the oven. The eggs will take 12 minutes to cook soft. Serve with slices of wholemeal (wholewheat) bread.

Teacakes

I always have a dozen of these in the freezer which I buy from a traditional, old-fashioned bakery in the Rossendale Valley. As you approach the door the air is filled with those wonderful baking smells. (Their meat and potato pies are super, and I piggishly eat mine in the street as they are never the same reheated at home.) Teacakes can be served for a snack, can form part of a high tea, or can be packed, filled, for your guests to take out walking, fishing or to some sporty occasion.

The teacakes should be split, buttered liberally and filled generously. Cold scrambled eggs with some chopped grapes and nuts make an unusual filling. Leftover bacon, sausage and fried apple go well with a dollop of pickle, chutney or bottled sauce (go on, I'm sure you have a bottle somewhere in your larder), as do some leftover cold roast meats.

Wrap the filled teacakes in lettuce leaves and then put into clingfilm (plastic wrap) and a plastic bag. This way they retain their moistness. In fact, another favourite filling of mine is simply sliced tomatoes sprinkled with a little sugar and fresh mint, as they tend to go quite soggy!

Cold Toasted Sandwiches

These are like the American, two-layer, club sandwiches, with lettuce, tomato, radishes, spring onions (scallions) and crisps as garnish.

Thin sliced bread is best for this, and it should be toasted with the crusts on. When stock-piling, do not put the slices on top of each other or they can become slightly soft and soggy. I lay them up against a tin at an angle like dominoes. When sufficient slices are toasted, cut the crusts off (save them for savoury breadcrumbs, see page 24). You need three slices of toast for each sandwich.

Butter each slice on one side. Lay one slice down on the work surface, butter side up, and top with a little dry, crisp lettuce (iceberg) with the merest hint of French dressing (you don't want it to become soggy). Cover the lettuce with the first filling. Lightly season, then put on the next slice of toast, buttered side down. Butter the exposed top and add the second filling. Top off with the third buttered slice, buttered side down. Gently press down these layers, and carefully cut into four triangles, using a very sharp, serrated, carving knife.

These sandwiches can be made ahead of time and placed on plates, garnished and covered with clingfilm (plastic wrap).

Choose from some of the following filling ideas.

1. *Peanut butter with chicken bits on one layer, with very well grilled (broiled) bacon slices and a little tomato provençale (see page 52) on the other.*
2. *Cream cheese with chutney on one layer, then pickled onions and pickled walnuts, chopped, with a little bottled brown sauce on the other.*
3. *Cream or cottage cheese (the latter can be a little sloppy, but is less fattening!) on one layer, with fresh fruit coated with toasted sesame seeds on the other. Use sliced apples, segments of orange, slices of plum, stoned cherries or pipped grapes.*
4. *Any leftover salad can be used on one layer with peanut butter mixed with mayonnaise on the other. Some diced red (bell) peppers would provide colour, taste and texture.*
5. *Cottage or cream cheese mixed with a little runny honey on one layer, with capers and anchovies mixed with chopped hard-boiled eggs on the other.*

Beer-battered Fish with Chips (French Fries)

You don't necessarily have to have the luxury of a built-in deep-fryer in your kitchen as there are many good free-standing ones on the market. In sheer desperation a large saucepan with an insertable chip (French fry) basket does the job very well indeed! All depends on the type of frying fat or oil you use and without any doubt I prefer to do my chips in a saucepan as I can keep this constantly topped up with beef or duck 'dripping'. The fat should be clean.

For good chips you need good potatoes, and the best for deep-frying are Desirée (Kennebec), Golden Wonder, King Edwards or Majestic. The quantity here will provide six very generous portions and it is important that the chips are cut into even sizes (small or large according to personal taste.)

SERVES 6

6 × 100 g (4 oz) portions cod, hake or halibut

good oil or fat for frying

BEER BATTER

100 g (4 oz/¾ cup) plain (all-purpose) flour

a pinch of salt

a pinch of curry powder if you desire

2 eggs, separated

120 ml (8 tablespoons) beer

CHIPS

1.4 kg (3 lb) good chip (French fry) potatoes, peeled and cut into chips

To make the batter, place the sieved plain flour into a bowl with the salt (add the curry powder if you like), and make a well in the middle. Beat the egg yolks with the beer and add this to the well, and little by little beat in the flour until you have a smooth batter. Leave covered in a cool place for at least 30 minutes.

Meanwhile prepare the chips, and dry them very well.

Beat the egg whites until stiff and fold into the batter. Dip your prepared fish portions in this batter and fry off in the oil preheated to 176°C/350°F for 4 minutes on each side. Remove to a tray lined with kitchen paper towels. Fry the dry chips at the same temperature until nice and golden, then remove to kitchen paper towels and cover.

When you wish to serve, turn up the heat of the oil to 185°C/365°F and fry the fish for 4 minutes. Drain and keep warm. Turn the heat up again, to 190°C/375°F, and fry the chips for a further 3–4 minutes until quite crisp and brown. Serve the fish and chips immediately with sea salt and vinegar.

Sweet Roast Ham

To serve six happily, buy a ham of between 2.7 and 3.6 kg (6–8 lb) in weight. The secret is to soak it in cold water for several days, changing the water twice daily. I simply put it into the large saucepan I wish to cook it in, cover it with water and a lid, and leave it in the larder. It may be a bit of a bore emptying the water out and replenishing night and morning, but it's well worthwhile if you want a deliciously sweet ham at the end.

1 × 2.7 kg (6 lb) ham, soaked as
   above
90 ml (6 tablespoons) black
   treacle (molasses)
lots of cloves
900 ml (1½ pints/3¾ cups) lager

When the ham has been soaked as described, remove from the last soaking water and leave to one side. Add the treacle to the water in the large pan and bring to the boil. Place the ham in the boiling water, put the lid on, and simmer away for 2 hours.

Take out of the water and wait until it cools or goes cold. With a sharp knife remove the skin and then cut through the fat to make diamond shapes. Into each one of these you stick a clove.

When you want to roast, bring the lager to the boil and preheat the oven to 190°C/375°F/mark 5. Pour the boiling lager into a large roasting tin (baking pan), and place the ham on top. Cook, basting every 15 minutes, for 1 hour. The ham can be served hot, but it is equally delicious cold, and served at high tea, supper or a picnic.

Overleaf: a summery high tea of Smoked Haddock Chowder with Baked Egg (page 86), Sweet Roast Ham (above) and chutneys, buttered wholemeal bread and Home-made Lemon Curd (page 154).

Salads

Salads can either be simple or simply splendid. I prefer the latter as virtually all that is needed is a vivid imagination! With that, plus a few basic ingredients in the house, you can make salads to please the most fastidious of guests, whether to accompany a light lunch, to take on a picnic, to have as a course like the French do at dinner, or for a tasty and healthy addition to a groaning high-tea table. I prefer to serve most salads in individual *wooden salad bowls (imported from the Far East, quite inexpensive, and which seem to improve with the years rather than deteriorate). This means that there is no need for polite small talk or passing large salad bowls around at the table: you can all simply get on with the job of* eating!

Provided you never add the French dressing (cold or hot) until just before serving, salads can be assembled a few hours ahead of time; covered in clingfilm (plastic wrap) and left somewhere cool, they come to no harm whatsoever. (If you're taking salads on a picnic, take them, covered in clingfilm (plastic wrap), in the wooden bowls – which won't break! – and the French dressing separately in its screw-top jar.)

The first thing I do before starting to assemble my salads is to place the merest drop of my favourite oil – walnut – in the base of each bowl, and this I rub right up the sides. I then put a ½ peeled clove of fresh garlic into each bowl and pound it quite hard with my pestle until it is really mushy. I rub this all over the inside of the bowl, then get rid of most of it by lightly wiping it out with a kitchen paper towel.

Then I start to arrange the base *of each salad, the lettuce or salad leaves. There are so many varieties of basic salad leaves around these days, one of the better aspects of the last few years of catering, so don't just go for the Webbs. Iceberg lettuces are a particularly good buy as they have such a long shelf-life in the fridge. When I use these, I cut wedges out and paint the two exposed sides with a little French dressing, cover with clingfilm (plastic wrap), and return to the fridge where they keep for 7–10 days. Oakleaf lettuces look very pretty, and lamb's lettuce is on the market most of the year now. Radicchio adds a dazzling colour to any salad. Lay your chosen leaves all around the base and edge of each bowl, to resemble the inside of a tulip flower, and then start putting your salad fillings inside. Sprigs of watercress and a sprinkling of mustard and cress are good, as are dandelion leaves and young spring nettles! Choose the* centre *of your salad from some of the salad combinations following.*

French Dressing

It is the dressing, however, that will make most salads memorable and believe it or not, as I've said many times before, the most important thing needed for this is your finger! All the time you are whizzing your mixture in the liquidizer, you keep on stopping the machine, and sticking your finger in to see if the flavour takes your fancy. The basic that I use is below, but you can also add bacon or duck fat, honey, 15 ml (1 tablespoon) of raspberry vinegar (what a potency this has even in the French dressing quantity below), the jelly at the base of your dripping bowl . . . . One or other will eventually give you just the flavour that you crave! See also the individual recipes for some possible further additions.

MAKES 900 ml (1½ pints/3¾ cups) BASIC DRESSING
600 ml (1 pint/2½ cups) good olive oil
150 ml (¼ pint/⅔ cup) white wine vinegar
1 teaspoon each of dry English mustard powder, salt and soft brown sugar
150 ml (¼ pint/⅔ cup) expensive oil such as hazelnut, walnut or almond

Simply mix together in the liquidizer and then store in a screw-top jar in the fridge. Remember to shake well before use.

Mushroom and Walnut

225 g (8 oz/4 cups) mushroom caps, peeled and sliced
3 tablespoons sour cream
30 ml (2 tablespoons) snipped chives
12 walnuts, coarsely chopped
2 oranges
150 ml (¼ pint/⅔ cup) home-made French dressing

Mix the mushrooms, cream, chives and walnuts together and pile on top of the salad leaves in the bowls. Use the finely grated rind from both oranges as a mini dollop on the top, and mix the juice of one into the French dressing.

Overleaf: two high tea salads, to be served with Mini Wheatmeal Loaves (page 69): on the left, Cottage Cheese with Grapes, Red (Bell) Pepper and Apple; on the right, Watercress, Orange and Walnut with Bacon Bits (both on page 98).

Egg, Chive and Sour Cream

12 hard-boiled eggs, chopped
90 ml (6 tablespoons) finely
    snipped chives
180 ml (12 tablespoons) sour
    cream

Simply mix together and pile on top of the salad leaves.

Apple, Lime, Grape and Mushroom

2 Granny Smith apples, cored and
    thinly sliced
juice and freshly grated rind of 2
    fresh limes
100 g (4 oz/2 cups) mushroom
    caps, peeled and thinly sliced
90 ml (6 tablespoons) natural
    (plain) yoghurt
fresh herbs, finely chopped
6 grapes per person, whole if
    seedless, halved and pipped if
    larger

Marinate the apple slices in the lime juice and rind for at least 3 hours. At the same time, marinate the thinly sliced mushroom caps in the yoghurt with the fresh herbs. The apples take on a distinctive and quite different flavour, which generally causes much comment!

Pile the apple and mushroom slices and the grapes, along with any remaining lime juice and yoghurt on to the salad leaves in the bowls.

Courgettes (Zucchini) in Orange Juice Topped with Sour Cream and Mint

450 g (1 lb) courgettes (zucchini),
    topped, tailed and wiped
juice and finely grated rind of
    2 oranges
6 tablespoons sour cream
chopped fresh mint to taste

Marinate the courgettes (zucchini) in the orange juice and rind for at least 4 hours. Wring them dry in a clean teatowel, otherwise they are very mushy. Divide between the bowls on top of the salad leaves and top each with a tablespoon of sour cream and some chopped mint. The flavour of the mint is often enhanced if, when chopping, you add a little soft brown sugar. (I also occasionally add a Granny Smith apple, that has been peeled, cored and finely diced.)

French Bean and New Potato with Mustard Dressing

It is important that you purchase the imported Kenyan (or other) French beans as they are matchstick like, as thin as thin can be, and only about 10–12.5 cm (4–5 inch) in length. Start preparing this salad a day in advance.

225 g (8 oz) matchstick French
   beans, topped and tailed

salt

a knob of butter

150 ml ($\frac{1}{4}$ pint/$\frac{2}{3}$ cup) home-made
   French dressing

15 ml (1 tablespoon) (at least)
   Dijon mustard

6 walnut-sized new potatoes,
   scrubbed and cooked (see page
   20)

*P*lunge the prepared beans into 600 ml (1 pint/$2\frac{1}{2}$ cups) boiling salted water and cook for 2 minutes only. Drain and return to the pan with a good knob of butter to dry off. Mix the French dressing with the mustard and pour over the beans. Marinate for at least 24 hours.

When you want to serve the salad, slice the cold potatoes thinly and arrange over the salad leaves in the bowls. Arrange the marinated beans on top of this, in a criss-cross pattern, making sure that you pour all the dressing over the individual bowls.

Broad Beans with Bacon Bits

at least 900 g (2 lb) broad (fava)
   beans

a pinch of salt

5 ml (1 teaspoon) lemon juice

350 g (12 oz) bacon, rinded

*P*reparing fresh broad (fava) beans is a tiresome task but as the season is so short, I begrudge not one minute taken to make this dish. I simply cannot tell you the quantities of fresh broad beans you should purchase as, oh, how they vary when you start to pod them. I know that the 900 g (2 lb) quoted above is the absolute minimum you will have to buy to feed six.

Remove the beans from their pods and place in a pan with 600 ml (1 pint/$2\frac{1}{2}$ cups) water, the salt and fresh lemon juice. Bring to the boil, then simmer for 5 minutes. Strain and leave to go cold. Take each individual bean and painstakingly tear off the stalk end and squeeze the little rich green inside bean out. This takes *ages*!

Meanwhile, cut the bacon into very small pieces with scissors or a knife. Fry these pieces until all the fat has run out, and the bacon bits are hard and crisp (you could have added some oil). Mix the beans with the warm fat and bacon bits (it's important that the fat and bits are *warm*), and pile on top of the salad leaves in the bowls. Accompany with thin slices of buttered brown bread, and I bet you even your most sophisticated guest will use some to wipe the bowl clean!

Radish, Apple and Celeriac (Celery Root)

450 g (1 lb) celeriac (celery root),
    washed, peeled and coarsely
    grated
2 Granny Smith apples, cored and
    finely grated
150 ml ($\frac{1}{4}$ pint/$\frac{2}{3}$ cup) sour cream
15 ml (1 tablespoon) horseradish
    cream
1 bunch radishes, topped, tailed
    and very thinly sliced

Mix the grated celeriac (celery root) and apple with the sour cream and horseradish cream, and pile on to the salad leaves in the individual bowls. Arrange the radish slices in circles around each bowl so that they resemble a kind of flower.

Watercress, Orange and Walnut with Bacon Bits

at least 175 g (6 oz) bacon, rinded
15 ml (1 tablespoon) walnut oil
1 bunch watercress, trimmed
3 oranges, segmented (see
    page 15)
75 g (3 oz/$\frac{3}{4}$ cup) walnuts,
    chopped

Chop the bacon and cook in the walnut oil as on page 97 until crisp, and all the fat has come out. (This can be done earlier in the day, and then the bacon bits and fat reheated just prior to serving.)

Mix the watercress, orange segments and walnuts together and pile on to the salad leaves in the bowls. Pour over the warmed bacon bits and the fat.

Cottage Cheese with Grapes, Red (Bell) Pepper and Apple

Cottage cheese doesn't usually get the thumbs up from me, but when I go on a diet (one week prior to going on holiday normally, so that I have no conscience about making a pig of myself when away), I will have it in the fridge. Simply place 25 ml (1 generous tablespoon) of cottage cheese on your prepared leaves in each bowl and then scatter the outer leafy circle with halved pipped grapes. Scatter diced red (bell) pepper over the cheese. At the last moment wedge thin apple slices (the skin still on, to give more colour) into the cheese. A mere sprinkling of paprika gives the whole thing a lift.

Other Salad Ideas

The ideas left are more specific, but the following may inspire you as well. They could be added to the individual salad bowl concoctions – ie the red kidney beans – but the mangetout (snow peas) and tomato salads are better served separately.

Firstly, there is hardly one of these salads above that wouldn't be rendered even tastier by having a twirl of cheese and herb pâté (see page 148) piped on the base under the leaves, or on the top at the last minute.

Mangetout could be stuffed with cheese and herb pâté too. Top and tail medium mangetout and then, using a very sharp pointed knife, open up three-quarters of one side. Pipe in some pâté through a thin nozzle, and they look lovely served with a salad, or served with pre-dinner drinks.

Whenever I get my first annual leaves of basil (basilicum), I can't resist making a simple tomato and basil salad. I dribble pure walnut oil over just as I am about to serve, and then grate some fresh Parmesan on top at the table. You could also skin tomatoes, thinly slice them and fan them out into a circle on a plate. Sprinkle some soft brown sugar on top followed by a generous sprinkling of finely chopped fresh herbs. Finish off with some toasted almonds. If you make a circle of tomatoes, the middle looks very attractive filled with watercress heads.

Marinated kidney beans are a good salad addition, and give colour and texture (as well as protein of course). If you use dried beans, soak them well, and then cook, making sure you first boil them for 10 minutes. But it's much easier to use canned. Buy a can of a reputable brand, open, and put the beans into a plastic strainer. Hold for several minutes under a slow running cold tap to let the cold water run through and rinse them thoroughly. Place on kitchen paper towels to dry, then put them into a bowl and cover with French dressing. Leave covered in the fridge for 2–3 days. They absorb some of the dressing and are very tasty.

Beansprouts can be marinated in French dressing too, becoming very much tastier. They're delicious, drained, served with the vegetable casserole on page 121.

I like to use radicchio in salads, as it looks very pretty in the dish, but it's very bitter (because of its chicory parentage). To counteract this, I always make sure that the French dressing is fairly sweet, mixing in some runny honey or soft brown sugar when I'm whizzing the dressing round in the liquidizer. To give added sweetness, texture and taste, I add about four fresh orange segments per person, a handful of roughly chopped pecans and the odd spray of watercress to provide a contrast in colour.

SUPPERS

Suppers can vary enormously in content and aim. They can be quite high tea-ish (as in Scotland) with cups of tea, a light savoury course and sweet cakes to follow; or they can be like a miniature dinner. They can be a light evening meal after a substantial lunch, or they can be a late snack after something like an early high tea. A supper is what you would serve if your guests didn't arrive in time for dinner – very welcome on a Friday, say, after a weary week and a long journey – and you would pre-prepare a supper ready for consumption after a Saturday night excursion to theatre or concert (the casserole dishes would be particularly useful here: set your oven timer).

Although many of the recipes following are fairly substantial, the emphasis should always be on a fairly *light* meal – supper is nearer bedtime than any other meal – and therefore should only consist of one or two courses. A hot soup with some delicious home-made bread (the individual loaves on page 69, for instance) or a baked potato followed by some cheese, fruit, or a lightish pudding, would be a good balance. And I would always offer a tea afterwards – of the new teas available, passionfruit and mango are my favourites.

Even though supper is in essence a fairly informal meal, I would still always go for atmosphere and glamour. I would set the table with simple place settings and enhance them with some flowers. I often use a cake stand on which I place a foil cooking/freezer dish holding some floral foam; I trail greenery around the whole thing to disguise the foil and then do the simplest arrangement of hedgerow flowers in the middle. I stand tall candles in the middle and these are always *lit*. Nursery nightlights can also look very attractive scattered around the table, adding to the atmosphere and, oh yes, don't forget about the music. Something smooth and soothing. With all this as background, practically anything can be served with confidence and aplomb!

Before you go to bed, make sure you have the trays set for morning coffee or tea, and that new guests know where they and all the accessories are. (Some kind person might even bring *you* up a cup of tea!) Make sure too that guests know where rooms are, where the bathroom is and how everything works – the electric blanket say. If it's cold, they might want a hot water bottle (if you haven't got electric blankets, obviously), and the last thing I might do for guests at night is offer a thermos flask of a bedtime milky drink (which I've made hours before).

Try not to be too late going to bed on a Friday, as Saturday will be busy, aiming for a lazy day on the Sunday before the house party breaks up.

Curried Leftover Vegetable Soups

During the course of the week get into the habit of cooking just that little bit extra of fresh vegetables and when they are cold, pile them into an airtight container and leave in the fridge. It matters not what vegetables you use (root ones are the best) as whilst the basic veg gives the goodness, it is the curry powder or paste that provides the dominant flavouring.

You simply need 600 ml (1 pint/2½ cups) good chicken stock along with the same amount of cold milk. Add this liquid to the vegetables – you'll need about 900 g (2 lb) – along with the curry powder, paste or other flavourings, and liquidize the whole lot. Pass through a sieve into a saucepan and taste. Experiment with the curry powder or paste to get the flavour that you like best, but I find 30 ml (2 tablespoons) powder suits me down to the ground.

When the sieved soup is heated, ready to be served, I top it with a thick layer of toasted desiccated (shredded) coconut and a few sultanas (white raisins) or slices of banana. As soup is a favourite supper dish of mine, I make it the 'main course'. I serve it in some very large pot bowls and have little dishes of garnishes on the table which you could use instead of the suggested additions above: double (heavy) cream, tiny croûtons, skinned and very finely chopped tomato, finely chopped onion, cubed avocado, chopped dates, snipped chives, chopped toasted nuts, yoghurt, chopped cucumber in a little tarragon vinegar, diced apple in lime juice or even crunched crisps (potato chips).

Overleaf: if you don't have time to cook, what could be simpler than bread and cheese followed by Boiled Loaf (page 69), berries and whipped cream for an easy supper.

Lentil Soup

This is a filling and satisfying soup for a cold evening. Garnished with sliced smoked sausage and roughly diced salami, and accompanied by thick, well buttered slices of wholemeal (whole wheat) bread, it will warm the cockles of your heart.

SERVES 6

450 g (1 lb) lentils

1.8 litres (3 pints/$7\frac{1}{2}$ cups) beef stock

1 cooked ham bone

2 small pig's trotters (feet), split down the middle

100 g (4 oz/$\frac{3}{4}$ cup) celery, trimmed and diced

1 medium onion, peeled and chopped

4 tomatoes, quartered

2 medium potatoes, peeled and roughly chopped

a pinch of freshly grated nutmeg

freshly ground black pepper and other seasonings to taste

Wash the lentils well in a sieve, drain several times and leave covered with 600 ml (1 pint/$2\frac{1}{2}$ cups) cold water overnight.

Drain and put into a clean saucepan covered with fresh water. Bring to the boil, simmer for 10 minutes, then drain. Return to the saucepan with all the other soup ingredients and bring back to the boil. Slowly simmer for 2 hours.

Remove the ham bone and trotters (feet) and liquidize the soup. Pass through a coarse sieve and adjust the seasoning to your own personal taste. A little added Worcestershire sauce, salt, sugar or a pinch of mustard will bring it round to suit your palate.

Serve in large heated bowls garnished with thinly sliced smoked sausage and diced salami. Leave the balance on the stove and have to hand a soup ladle, so that everybody can help themselves to seconds.

Vegetable Broth

If you are cooking chicken for six guests one weekend, you can use the carcasses of the two you will have had to cook to make a stock for the next weekend entertaining session. When ready, freeze it in ice-cube trays. A stock pot can be left simmering away in a cool kitchen for days but it needs two at least. The roasted bones from the chickens are broken up and placed in a thick-bottomed saucepan, covered with cold water and then the pan is left to simmer, never boil, for 48 hours. It needs some vegetable flavouring though, and every single time you have a stock pot on, whatever you are doing, constantly ask yourself "Will the scraps go in the stock pot?" You can use the outer leaves of lettuce, the base stalks and leaves of celery and the skins of garlic cloves; even the tops of radishes and stalks from tomatoes will all eventually contribute some flavour to the stock. Cast your eye on the saucepan from time to time and, as the water cooks away condensing the flavour and extracting

*every drop of goodness from the ingredients, you simply pour on more cold water –
and add some more scraps – and let it continue to cook. It might look a little
scummy on the top but don't worry. Pass through a strainer into a container and
when cold either refrigerate or freeze. (If you want to have an emergency supply for
small quantities, freeze in ice-cube trays and when solid pop the cubes out into
plastic bags.) But now for the soup itself.*

SERVES 6
1.2 litres (2 pints/5 cups) home-
  made chicken stock
900 g (2 lb) assorted vegetables,
  prepared (see method)
90 ml (6 tablespoons) double
  (heavy) cream
freshly chopped herbs

The vegetables can be a mixture of evenly diced root vegetables, some tiny cauliflower and broccoli florets, some fresh garden peas, and some small chunky wedges of garden runner beans – anything available and fresh. All you do is simply bring your stock up to a simmer, then pop in all the vegetables and cook for 20 minutes until the veg are slightly *al dente* (in other words, crisp). Stir in the cream and a generous sprinkling of herbs (and grated cheese if you like). Serve with buttered fingers of hot toast or thick slices of wholemeal (whole wheat) bread.

Beef Tomatoes Filled with Peas

*The beef tomatoes for this must be quite firm and remember to put the insides into
your stockpan.*

SERVES 6
6 large beef tomatoes, approx.
  1.8 kg (4 lb) weight in total
salt and freshly ground black
  pepper
6 small knobs of butter
6 teaspoons chopped fresh herbs
675 g (1½ lb) frozen peas,
  defrosted
6 sprigs fresh mint

Wipe the tomatoes clean with a damp cloth and then put them on your work surface, stalk side down. Slice two-thirds of the way across just down from the top to make a 'lid'. Scoop out the centre of the tomato using a spoon or Parisian scoop. Season the inside of each and add a knob of butter. Mix the chopped herbs with the peas and spoon into the cavities, then place the tomatoes in a cooking dish. Put a little water in the base, and warm through at 180°C/350°F/ mark 4 for 15 minutes. Serve garnished with a sprig of fresh mint.

*Overleaf: a comforting supper in front of the fire: steaming
Lentil Soup (opposite) accompanied by buttered Wheatmeal
Scones (page 81).*

Savoury Baked Potatoes

Each person should have a good sized potato, but because of the quantity of sea salt required, it's not economical to prepare potatoes for less than two. They make a very good stand-by supper dish for family or weekend guests and can help you use up all sorts of bits and pieces left over in the fridge. They can, in fact, be precooked in the morning (or the night before), and finished off for 30 minutes before serving, which makes them a handy recipe to have up your sleeve. And I have never heard of a soul who turned up their nose at a good baked spud!

SERVES 6

6 potatoes, each at least 225 g
  (8 oz) in weight
lots of sea salt
75 g (3 oz/⅓ cup) butter
175 g (6 oz/1½ cups) Cheddar
  cheese, grated
6 bacon rashers

Preheat the oven to 220°C/425°F/mark 7, and scrub the potatoes clean. Dry them well on kitchen paper and place on a generous bed of sea salt in a roasting tin (baking pan). Bake in the oven for 1¼ hours. Remove and, as they're cooling, split in two lengthwise and scoop out the lovely fluffy middles. Put in a bowl and add the butter and cheese. Grill (broil) the bacon until crisp and then dice into tiny pieces (or, better still, finely chop and then fry until crisp). Add to the potato mixture. Pile the mixture back into the potato skins and, 30 minutes before you need them, return to the oven and cook for 30 minutes.

There are many different fillings you can use instead of the cheese and bacon, but always use 75 g (3 oz/⅓ cup) butter per 6 potatoes.

1. Chopped celery and apple with grated cheese and some skinned chopped tomatoes.
2. Mashed sardines with tomato provençale (see page 52).
3. Any leftover Bolognese sauce with extra fried onion.
4. Leftover peas or sweetcorn (corn on the cob) mixed with mustard, butter and cheese – and why not a little chutney?
5. Minced (ground) cold ham or chicken with plenty of fresh herbs and a little double (heavy) cream or top of milk.
6. Fried mushrooms, kidney and sliced sausages.
7. Nuts, cheese and chutney with a little onion and red (bell) pepper marmalade (see page 153).
8. Crunchy peanut butter with whole hazelnuts and chopped chives.

9. Bacon or duck fat can be substituted for the butter, with the pickings of chicken or duck carcasses along with any baked skin.
10. Any leftover bits of fish with some anchovy essence and a little yoghurt.
11. Any leftover vegetables can be finely diced and combined with a little chutney or curry powder and lightly beaten egg.
12. Raw grated radish, carrot and turnip with a touch of horseradish cream and lots of herbs.

Fried Ham and Cheese Sandwich

All the recipes in this book are for six, but here is one for one *only. We all know what it is to be confronted with an unexpected visitor or somebody needing sustenance* there and then *who can't wait for a proper meal – perhaps you might have house guests who suddenly decide they want to go to the cinema and miss supper and comes the question "Is there something we can have in a jiffy?" The answer is this sandwich which, in Minim's restaurant in Paris (the poor relation of Maxim's), is called Croque Monsieur in a slightly milder version.*

SERVES 1
50 g (2 oz/4 tablespoons) butter
2 thin bread slices, crusts removed
1 slice ham or 2 slices chicken or turkey
50 g (2 oz/½ cup) Cheddar cheese, grated
1 egg
salt and freshly ground black pepper
freshly chopped herbs

Melt half the butter in a frying pan (skillet) and fry one side of each slice or round of bread until brown. Remove from the pan and lay the uncooked side down. Place the ham, chicken or turkey slices on top, cut so that they don't overlap the perimeter of the bread, and sprinkle over the grated cheese. Press the other slice, fried side down, sharply on top of the filling. Beat the egg with a little salt and pepper and coat the outside of the sandwich with this. Melt the remaining butter in the frying pan, fry the sandwich on each side until golden, and serve immediately, sprinkled with the herbs.

Overleaf: a hearty Vegetable Broth (page 104) sprinkled with grated cheese and accompanied by hot French bread, makes a healthy supper when followed by fresh fruit.

Cauliflower Cheese on Onion and Red (Bell) Pepper Marmalade

This is an uncommon or garden cauliflower cheese. The sauce is very rich, and the onion and red (bell) pepper marmalade adds an interesting tang.

SERVES 6

1 large cauliflower, weighing
   about 800 g (1¾ lb)

salt

90 ml (6 tablespoons) onion and
   red (bell) pepper marmalade
   (see page 153)

CHEESE SAUCE

600 ml (1 pint/2½ cups) milk

50 g (2 oz/4 tablespoons) butter

50 g (2 oz/⅓ cup) plain flour

freshly ground black pepper

¼ teaspoon dry English mustard
   powder

100 g (4 oz/1 cup) strong Cheddar
   cheese, grated

First of all soak the cauliflower, head down, in a bowl of salted water (to bring out any bugs which may be hidden in the florets). Fit a colander snugly over a large pan of boiling salted water, place the prepared cauliflower (head down) in this, and cover with the lid. Steam for 10 minutes when it will still be nice and crisp, ready for the next stage. Cut into large florets.

Line the base of a large oval, ovenproof dish with the marmalade and arrange the florets (flower side upmost) on this.

To make the cheese sauce, you will need two saucepans. Warm through the milk in one. Melt the butter in another, then add the flour and cook, beating quite vigorously against the sides of the saucepan. Add the warmed milk, a quarter at a time, and really beat the mixture smooth before adding any more milk. When all has been added, simmer for 10 minutes at least in order to cook out the taste of the flour. Add the grated cheese and cook until smooth, stirring continuously.

Pour the sauce over the cauliflower in the dish and heat through in the preheated oven at 180°C/350°F/mark 4 for 20 minutes. Finish off under the grill (broiler) to get a brown, crisp topping.

A Trio of Vegetable Purées

This is a 'cowboy' way of serving three vegetables with no effort at all when you are entertaining at the weekend.

During the course of the week, when you are preparing and serving root vegetables, simply cook more than you need and when cold put the extra into airtight containers. For a decent serving, I would suggest you ensure you have 225 g (8 oz/1 cup) extra of each of cooked parsnips, carrots and turnips.

When you want to assemble the dish, use a fairly large oval ovenproof, see-through dish, or six individual ramekin dishes. Butter and season the dish or dishes. Place each vegetable in turn into the food processor along with 75 ml ($\frac{1}{8}$ pint/$\frac{1}{4}$ cup) double (heavy) or single (light) cream, and whizz around until well blended. Pass through a sieve into three separate bowls. For added flavour you can add a good pinch of grated nutmeg to the parsnip, some finely chopped preserved (candied) ginger to the carrot, and a touch of horseradish cream to the turnips. These three are then built up in layers, with the parsnip in the middle obviously, topped with some savoury breadcrumbs (see page 24), and covered with clingfilm (plastic wrap).

When you wish to cook, place the small ramekins or the one dish in a roasting tin (baking pan), half-fill the latter with enough boiling water to come half-way up the dish or dishes, and place in the oven preheated to 180°C/350°F/mark 4. The small dishes take 15 minutes to heat through, and the large single dish, 30–40 minutes.

Duck Liver in Bacon served with Redcurrant, Mustard and Orange Sauce

A quick and interesting snack which would please the most fastidious of guests...

SERVES 6
6 large fresh ducks' livers
freshly ground black pepper
6 rashers smoked bacon, rinded
SAUCE
8 tablespoons redcurrant jelly
$\frac{1}{2}$ teaspoon English mustard
juice and finely grated rind of 1
   orange

Cut open the duck livers and lightly wash them, taking care to snip away and discard any yellowish bits. Dry them well on kitchen paper towels and grind a little black pepper over them. Roll each duck liver up in a rasher of bacon and hold together with a wooden cocktail stick. Cook for 15 minutes in an oven pre-heated to 200°C/400°F/mark 6.

Meanwhile, make the sauce. Simply put the ingredients into a small saucepan and leave to simmer for 5 minutes. Beat to make sure the mustard is evenly distributed throughout the liquid, and then pour over the livers in a dish. Serve with a grilled tomato and a spoonful of peas for colour, or even a potato rissole made from leftover mashed potato. An added garnish could be toasted sesame seeds sprinkled over the top.

Overleaf: Calvados Apple Duck Liver Pâté (page 117) with Melba toast or home-made cheesey biscuits, followed by good farmhouse cheese and celery, makes a delicious supper.

Plaited Pastry Loaf

This is a down-to-earth version of the classical Boeuf en Croûte, and as it can be done way ahead of time (it comes to no harm whatsoever in the freezer provided it is frozen with the pastry uncooked*), it's just a matter of glazing it and popping it into the preheated oven. Your guests will gasp with joy at the look of it, and hopefully will enjoy the various fillings that can be used.*

450 g (1 lb) puff pastry
filling of choice (see below)
1 egg, lightly beaten with a drop
   of water

*B*ring the puff pastry round to room temperature and then roll it to 3 mm ($\frac{1}{8}$ inch) thickness on a lightly floured work surface to a 37.5 × 30 cm (15 × 12 inch) rectangle.

Pile the filling in the centre of the rectangle in a rectangular shape, leaving good borders all round. On the long sides, cut in at an angle two-thirds towards the filling, to make 'plaits'. Paint these with the egg wash, then bring the two uncut end pieces up over the filling. Working from the end away from you, bring the plaits up individually, left/right, left/right, etc., until all is done. Paint again with the egg wash, wrap in grease-proof paper and foil, and freeze.

When you want to cook, bring the loaf round to room temperature, glaze again if you like, and bake for 40 minutes in an oven preheated to 220°C/425°F/mark 7. A reduced cream sauce will enhance this dish, and takes no time at all to make.

Savoury Mince (Ground Beef or Lamb)

450 g (1 lb) savoury mince (see
   page 118)

*F*ollow the method as described above.

Salmon, Egg, Rice and Peas

100 g (4 oz/1 cup) cooked rice
350 g (12 oz) salmon, cooked and
   flaked
50 g (2 oz/$\frac{1}{2}$ cup) frozen peas,
   defrosted
2 hard-boiled eggs, finely
   chopped

*S*imply mix together and encase in the pastry.

Halibut, (Bell) Pepper and Mushroom

100 g (4 oz/1 cup) red (bell)
  pepper, seeded and diced
350 g (12 oz) halibut, flaked
100 g (4 oz/2 cups) mushroom
  caps, finely sliced

*S*imply mix together and encase in the pastry.

Curried Vegetable and Chutney

450 g (1 lb) root vegetables,
  chunkily chopped
chutney
curry powder

*F*ry the veg chunks as for the vegetable casserole on page 121, then mix with some of your favourite chutney and curry powder to taste. Encase in the pastry.

Calvados Apple Duck Liver Pâté

Served chilled, in individual ramekins (although it can be moulded in one large dish), this is a good starter for a supper accompanied by thin toast and lots of butter. It's good enough for a dinner starter too, especially if you tart it up with some more redcurrant jelly melted with a little Calvados and used as a glaze.

SERVES 6
100 g (4 oz/½ cup) butter
1 apple, peeled and segmented
175 g (6 oz) onions, peeled and
  finely chopped
450 g (1 lb) duck livers
75 ml (5 tablespoons) Calvados
75 ml (5 tablespoons) cider (hard
  cider)
30 ml (2 tablespoons) redcurrant
  jelly
10 ml (2 teaspoons) freshly
  chopped marjoram leaves
salt and freshly ground black
  pepper

*H*eat half the butter in a pan and cook the apple and onion until soft. Transfer to your food processor. Add the balance of the butter to the pan and turn up the heat. Seal the cleaned prepared duck (or chicken) livers, then transfer them to the processor as well.

Turn up the heat under the buttery pan, pour in the Calvados, and flame it. Add the cider and redcurrant jelly, then turn down heat, mix well with a wooden spoon and reduce to about 2 tablespoons. Add this with the marjoram and salt and pepper to taste to the processor, and blend. Pass through a plastic sieve into a bowl, then divide between six ramekins. Chill.

Macaroni Beef or Lamb Savoury

This is a dish my grandmother used to cook on a Tuesday to use up the tiny amounts of meat left over from the Sunday joint. (The majority of that meat would have gone into my grandad's 'bait' to take to the shipyard on Monday, then some would have been served on Monday night in very thin slices accompanied by delicious chips/French fries cooked in beef dripping or duck fat.) Any still leftover after all this would be mixed with macaroni and onions with the part-cooked macaroni seared until brown (to make it look meaty). I, of course, have adapted and updated the recipe and made it slightly more lavish!

SERVES 6

100 g (4 oz/1 cup) packet
  macaroni
salt
25 g (1 oz/2 tablespoons) butter
30–45 ml (2–3 tablespoons)
  freshly chopped parsley

**SAVOURY MINCE (ground
beef or lamb)**

50 g (2 oz/4 tablespoons) butter
175 g (6 oz) onions, peeled and
  finely diced
2 garlic cloves, peeled and
  crushed with 5 ml (1 teaspoon)
  salt
675 g (1½ lb) uncooked beef or
  lamb, minced (ground)
300 ml (½ pint/1¼ cups) tomato
  provençale (see page 52)
freshly ground black pepper

To make the savoury mince (ground meat), melt the butter in a large frying pan (skillet) and then fry the onions and garlic gently until golden brown. Add the minced (ground) meat and cook for 30 minutes until well browned. Add the tomato provençale and some pepper, and set aside until needed.

Meanwhile, cook the macaroni according to the instructions on the packet, rinse under cold running water and drain very well. Put back in the pan over heat to dry, and you may even want to use kitchen paper towels to make it as dry as possible. Melt the 25 g (1 oz/2 tablespoons) butter in a frying pan, turn up the heat, and sear the dry macaroni until browned. Remove from the pan and add to the savoury mince. Stir together for about 10 minutes, then serve, garnished with the chopped parsley.

(Make on Friday)

Beef & Simmers
Casserole

Herbed Beef Guinness Casserole

Casseroles are ideal for weekend entertaining, and this one is particularly tasty and satisfying for a cold evening. It can be made well in advance and reheated. Serve with simple mashed potatoes, and a green vegetable.

SERVES 6

900 g (2 lb) good stewing beef, cut into 2.5 cm (1 inch) cubes

75 g (3 oz/$\frac{1}{2}$ cup) seasoned flour

75 ml ($\frac{1}{8}$ pint/$\frac{1}{4}$ cup) olive oil

75 g (3 oz/$\frac{1}{3}$ cup) butter

175 g (6 oz) smoked bacon, rinded and finely chopped

225 g (8 oz) button (pearl) onions, peeled

100 g (4 oz) each of carrots and turnips, peeled and finely diced

4 juicy garlic cloves, peeled and crushed with 5 ml (1 teaspoon) salt

30 ml (2 tablespoons) cooking brandy

15 ml (1 tablespoon) wine vinegar

15 ml (3 teaspoons) dried thyme

60 ml (4 tablespoons) freshly chopped parsley

2 bottles Guinness

100 g (4 oz/2 cups) mushrooms, wiped and thinly sliced

Lightly coat the beef cubes with seasoned flour. Heat the oil in a frying pan (skillet), melt the butter, and seal off the meat, a few cubes at a time. Drain on kitchen paper. Add the chopped bacon pieces to the pan and fry for a few minutes, then transfer to the draining paper.

Fry the whole onions, and diced carrots and turnip in the fat remaining in the pan, then drain on another tray lined with kitchen paper. Fry the garlic and salt paste for a few minutes.

Add the brandy to the pan, and stir around, scraping up all the bits of goodness adhering to the sides and bottom. Add the vinegar, thyme, parsley and Guinness, and mix well.

Put the meat and veg in a large heatproof casserole and pour over the liquid from the frying pan. Bring to the boil on top of the stove, mixing together well, then cover and cook in the preheated oven at 160°C/325°F/mark 3 for approximately 2 hours. About 15 minutes before the end of the cooking time, stir in the finely sliced mushrooms, and taste for seasoning.

Lamb Cutlets (Rib Lamb Chops) in Orange and Ginger with Pineapple

This is a very good dish for a weekend as it can be prepared well in advance; it also tastes even better if prepared up to the final stage, then frozen or chilled, and heated through for serving with the chopped fresh pineapple.

SERVES 6

12 lamb cutlets (rib lamb chops),
   trimmed

seasoned flour

60 ml (4 tablespoons) olive oil

100 g (4 oz/½ cup) butter

6 'nuts' preserved (candied)
   ginger, finely chopped

1 × 178 ml (6¼ fl oz) frozen
   concentrated orange juice

TO FINISH

6 slices fresh pineapple, cored
   and finely diced

Dry the cutlets on kitchen paper towels and coat lightly with the seasoned flour. Put 30 ml (2 tablespoons) of the olive oil into your frying pan (skillet) (just large enough to take three cutlets at a time), and when warm, add and melt 50 g (2 oz/4 tablespoons) of the butter. Seal three cutlets in the hot and hissing fat. When done, wipe out the frying pan and seal the other three cutlets in the remaining hot oil and butter. Place all six cutlets on the base of a casserole, with the preserved ginger.

Dilute the concentrated orange juice, but use *only two-thirds* of the water the directions state. Pour over the cutlets in the casserole, cover the whole thing with foil, and cook in the preheated oven at 110°C/225°F/mark ¼ for 2 hours. At this stage the dish can be frozen.

To reheat, set the oven at 200°C/400°F/mark 6 and heat through for 20–30 minutes, having added the finely diced fresh pineapple.

Breast of Chicken with Coconut Milk

This dish is sweetish in flavour, but the breasts are tenderly imbued with the coconut milk. In summer, garnish with a handful of seasonal summer berries – redcurrants on a sprig look sensational – or use canned stoned cherries in winter.

SERVES 6

6 chicken breasts

600 ml (1 pint/2½ cups) coconut
   milk

salt and freshly ground black
   pepper

15 ml (3 teaspoons) arrowroot

30 ml (2 tablespoons) white wine

Marinate the chicken breasts for at least 48 hours in the coconut milk, chilled, turning them twice a day.

When you wish to cook, bring the chicken breasts to the boil in the coconut milk, uncovered, on top of the stove. Season to taste, then put in a casserole, cover and bake in the preheated oven at 180°C/350°F/mark 4 for 35–40 minutes. Remove from the oven, take the breasts out and keep warm while you make the sauce.

Put the casserole with the juices and coconut milk on the hob again and simmer for about 10 minutes. Meanwhile, in a teacup, mix the arrowroot with the wine to a smooth paste. When the coconut milk is boiling, add the arrowroot mixture and stir vigorously. It will thicken up well.

Savoury Vegetable Casserole

This casserole is not strictly vegetarian as you have to use a chicken stock for added flavouring – but you could use a vegetable stock, or a thick cheese sauce as in the cauliflower cheese recipe on page 112. It can be prepared in advance and just warmed through prior to serving.

A delicious addition at the end is some beansprouts which have been marinated for an hour or so in French dressing (see page 93).

SERVES 6

1.4 kg (3 lb) basic root vegetables (equal quantities of white turnip, swede/rutabaga, carrot, parsnip, leek and celeriac/celery root), prepared and cut into fairly small equal cubes

100 g (4 oz/$\frac{1}{2}$ cup) butter

2 garlic cloves, peeled and crushed to a paste with 5 ml (1 teaspoon) salt

225 g (8 oz) onions, peeled and finely diced

600 ml (1 pint/2$\frac{1}{2}$ cups) chicken (or vegetable) stock or the cheese sauce on page 112

75 g (3 oz) savoury breadcrumbs (see page 24)

Melt half the butter and fry the garlic paste and the onions until golden. Remove from the pan with a slotted spoon and keep to one side.

Add the remaining butter to the pan when required and fry the vegetables in batches over a sizzling heat so that the cubes brown. Transfer to a casserole dish (the one I use is about 20 cm/8 inch in diameter, 10 cm/4 inch deep), stir everything together, and mix in the cooked onions and garlic. Pour over the chicken stock (or the cheese sauce) and cook in the preheated oven at 180°C/350°F/mark 4 for 45 minutes.

Take out and scatter the top with the savoury breadcrumbs and finish off under a very hot grill (broiler) to brown.

Overleaf: for a slightly more elaborate supper, serve slices of a Plaited Pastry Loaf (page 116), followed by Tangy Lemon Cream (page 124) and Shortbread Rounds (page 79).

Tangy Lemon Cream with Toasted Flaked Almonds

Put this sweet into six of your best red wine glasses and serve them on small plates with doyleys on; arrange a flower freshly picked from the garden down the left-hand side, with the teaspoon on the right. Offer thin shortbread rounds on page 79.

SERVES 6

15 g ($\frac{1}{2}$ oz) powdered gelatine

150 ml ($\frac{1}{4}$ pint/$\frac{2}{3}$ cup) dry white wine

3 eggs, separated

100 g (4 oz/$\frac{1}{2}$ cup) caster (superfine) sugar

3 lemons

300 ml ($\frac{1}{2}$ pint/1$\frac{1}{4}$ cups) double (heavy) cream

TO SERVE

toasted flaked almonds

Sprinkle the gelatine into a small saucepan and immediately pour on the dry white wine. Set aside.

Meanwhile warm the mixer bowl and into this put the egg yolks. Beat away until they are light and fluffy. Little by little, add the sugar.

In a saucepan, gently heat through the juice from all three of the lemons along with the finely grated rind of *one*. Slowly dribble this into the egg yolk mixture.

In a separate bowl, with the electric hand-whisk, beat the cream until batter consistency, and in yet another bowl, using clean beaters, beat the egg whites until stiff. Fold the cream into the egg yolk mixture and place the small saucepan with the gelatine and wine over the *lowest heat possible*. (Gelatine should never come in touch with a high heat otherwise it will simply coagulate and remain in the saucepan). When the mixture is perfectly clear, pass through a sieve into the egg yolk/cream mixture and incorporate, using a long-handled spoon. Fold in one-third of the beaten eggs, followed by the rest after they have been beaten stiff again (egg whites fall so quickly). Spoon out into the six glasses, cover and chill to set, about 2 hours. To serve, sprinkle with the toasted flaked almonds.

Raspberry Purée

Delicious with many poached fruits, in trifle (see page 61) or with a cream ice.

MAKES ABOUT 600 ml (1 pint/2$\frac{1}{2}$ cups)

675 g (1$\frac{1}{2}$ lb) fresh raspberries

175 g (6 oz/1$\frac{1}{2}$ cups) icing (confectioners') sugar

Simply process the raspberries and sugar in a food processor or liquidizer for about 4–6 minutes (you will be surprised at how tough those little seeds are), and then press through a plastic sieve. Chill or freeze.

Melon with Raspberry Purée

Purchase really fresh ripe melons for this dish even if you incur the temporary displeasure of your local vegetable man as you gently press the top and bottom of each melon to see if it 'gives', testing it for ripeness.

Top and tail each melon – Cantaloupe is best – and then cut in two and remove the seeds. If you have a Parisian scoop it is eye-appealing to scoop out little balls around the perimeter only, turn them upside down and put back in their holes. This can be done earlier and the melons left covered with clingfilm (plastic wrap).

Just prior to serving put 30 ml (2 tablespoons) of the raspberry purée in the well of each melon half (even better if you add a drop of brandy to the purée), and then scatter in any fresh summer berries you may have to hand.

Poached Spiced Peaches and Apricots

A weekend is helped along by a couple of bowls of partly cooked fruit, and if somebody needs a second pud with any meal it is a relatively simple task to tell them to go to the fridge and help themselves. They could also be served for breakfast with muesli (granola) or with whipped sweetened cream.

10 peaches
20 fresh apricots
900 g (2 lb) cube (lump) sugar
60 ml (4 tablespoons) white wine
   vinegar
allspice berries

The peaches and apricots need to be cooked separately in syrup, so prepare the latter first. Using two large metal ovenproof casseroles (I've got *one*, which has a deep lid that doubles as a second casserole), put in each 1.2 litres (2 pints/5 cups) water, with 450 g (1 lb/2¼ cups) sugar and 30 ml (2 tablespoons) white wine vinegar. Add 30 allspice berries to the syrup for the peaches, 20 to that for the apricots. Bring these two casseroles to the boil on the stove and keep simmering away (stirring from time to time with a wooden spoon) until all the sugar has dissolved and you have a syrup.

Preheat the oven to 180°C/350°F/mark 4 and put the peaches into their dish and the apricots into theirs. Put in the oven and cook the apricots for 20 minutes, the peaches for 30. Leave to cool.

When cool, carefully remove and discard the skins with a sharp knife. Return the fruits to their respective dishes of syrup and when cold put in the fridge.

DINNERS

This is the time when you can pull out all the stops and serve a full three courses, using all the skills at your disposal, and expending a little more energy than at any other time during the weekend. You'll notice, however, that most things can still have been prepared in advance to a certain extent – the marinating of meat, for instance – which means you 'work' during the week, and have less to do when you want to be with your guests. None of the recipes in this section, although slightly more elaborate and Miller Howe-ish, is difficult, and none will have you getting into a panic before the meal starts. Just the opposite, in fact! However, don't do any for the first time when you have guests, but try them all out on the family first, remembering that familiarity means a calm, confident cook who will be very much in control of the event.

And dinner should be an event! Use your best china and glasses, old family silver, and dine by candlelight, of course. (A tip here is to make certain your candles have spent at least a few hours in the freezer, and are brought out at the last minute. This way they won't drip all over your polished table surface or best cloth.) Spend some time in the afternoon making the table look extra special, check all the light bulbs, and see that you have some suitable background tapes which will cover up any possible lull in the conversation (this won't happen in *your* house). Double-check that you have all the necessary serving gear to hand in the kitchen and, most important of all, ensure that the kitchen is very tidy, allowing you lots of work space so that the evening can be stage-managed properly. I can't stress the importance of this enough.

I've divided the recipes into three-course dinners – four of them – but they could also be served as grand Sunday lunches instead, if that's how you want to organize your weekend meals. Still go to town with the table, with flowers and faultless organization – but you won't need the candles presumably!

I haven't given any vegetable recipes to accompany the main courses, but there are a few throughout other sections which would do – the vegetable purées and cauliflower cheese on page 112 for instance. Everything depends so much on the season, and what is fresh, delicious and available. I would always go for the simplest, though – equal sized dice or florets steamed with a little flavouring, or grated veg stir-fried in butter and oil with a little something extra scattered on top (toasted pine kernels, flaked almonds or bacon bits). There are a million possible variations to choose from and all you need is a little imagination. None of these should take longer than 10 minutes, being prepared and cooked at the very last minute – while the roast is resting, say.

Potatoes, too, depend on the season. In the summer, nothing could be better than new potatoes with butter and mint, and in winter, baked potatoes would be warming and satisfying (see page 108). Mashed potatoes don't need a recipe, but don't forget to add some butter and top of the milk, along with some freshly grated nutmeg, for the best possible flavour and consistency. Roast potatoes for an hour alongside your meat.

A salad, of course, is often the nicest way to accompany a main course, and you'll find a vast selection in the High Tea section. To make a meal even more splendid, you could serve a salad as a separate course before the meat, followed by some cheese and *then* the pud!

Tomato and Pernod Sorbet in Lightly Curried Tulip Case

Now don't raise your eyebrows and dismiss this sorbet, as it is one of the most popular served at Miller Howe, and one I often serve as a starter or a quickie between courses. It has to be made at least the day before so that is one job less on the day. The lightly curried tulip cases can be made in advance as well, and stored in an airtight tin (do this with great care to avoid crushing them). Use grapefruit – three of them – to mould the cases.

SERVES 6
SORBET
600 ml (1 pint/2½ cups) water
175 g (6 oz) cube (lump) sugar
1.4 kg (3 lb) tomatoes, skinned
   and seeded
60 ml (4 tablespoons) Pernod
TULIP CASE
100 g (4 oz/½ cup) caster
   (superfine) sugar
50 g (2 oz/⅓ cup) plain (all-
   purpose) flour, sieved
2.5 ml (½ teaspoon) curry powder
50 g (2 oz/4 tablespoons) butter,
   melted
2 egg whites

To make the sorbet, put the water and sugar into a saucepan, bring to the boil, then simmer, stirring from time to time to ensure the sugar dissolves, for 15 minutes. Leave to one side and when it is cold, freeze.

Bring the frozen stock syrup out of the freezer, and let it become slushy. Whisk in your processor until smooth, then add the tomatoes and Pernod. Blend well, then return to the dish and freeze.

To make the tulip cases, preheat the oven to 180°C/350°F/mark 4, and line a baking tray with excellent greaseproof (wax) paper. Have a palette knife to hand. Sieve the sugar, flour and curry powder into a bowl, then make a well in the centre. Put the melted butter in this well, and swiftly combine to a batter. Beat the egg whites stiff and fold carefully in.

Spoon 3 dessertspoons of the mixture out on to the prepared baking sheet (leaving lots of room around the dollops), and, using the palette knife, spread each one as thinly as possible. Put the trays in the oven and cook for 15 minutes, or until golden.

When cooked, remove the tray from the oven and leave for a few minutes for the biscuits to begin setting. Have the three grapefruit close at hand. Using the palette knife, carefully flick each 'pancake' over a grapefruit and then mould to a cup shape with your fingers. They become quite crisp quite quickly in a cool kitchen. Cook off a further three cases, mould similarly, and leave all six to become quite cold.

To serve, arrange the tulip cases on plates, and place a scoop of the sorbet in the middle (not too far in advance). Top with a sprig of mint.

Loin of Pork Marinated in Coconut Milk with Pineapple, and Coffee Cream Sauce

A touch of the exotic – or some people may well say simply over the top! The sweet richness of this dish is what is so wicked – but oh so wonderful. And what the hell, one can always go on that wretched diet on Monday!

SERVES 6

900 g (2 lb) loin of pork, weighed after boning and skinning

450 ml ($\frac{3}{4}$ pint/2 cups) coconut milk

300 ml ($\frac{1}{2}$ pint/1$\frac{1}{4}$ cups) dry white wine

6 fresh pineapple rings, cored

demerara (brown) sugar

fresh watercress

toasted desiccated (shredded) coconut (optional)

SAUCE

600 ml (1 pint/2$\frac{1}{2}$ cups) double (heavy) cream

a pinch of salt

45 ml (3 tablespoons) Camp (extra strong liquid) coffee

*M*arinate the well trimmed pork for at least 3 days in a mixture of the coconut milk and white wine, turning twice daily.

When you wish to cook, preheat the oven to 220°C/425°F/mark 7. Put 600 ml (1 pint/2$\frac{1}{2}$ cups) of the milk and wine mix into the base of the roasting tin (baking pan), place the meat in on top and roast for 1$\frac{1}{4}$ hours, basting occasionally.

Place the fresh pineapple rings on a well buttered baking sheet and sprinkle some demerara (brown) sugar over them. These will take 10 minutes to warm through whilst the loin is finishing cooking.

The light coffee cream sauce, which I like very much, is easy to make. Simply reduce the cream by half with the salt, then beat in the Camp (extra strong liquid) coffee.

Carve the meat in thickish slices then put a pineapple ring on top with watercress sprigs cascading out. Serve the sauce separately and, if you like, scatter some toasted desiccated (shredded) coconut over the meat and sauce.

Overleaf: Tomato and Pernod Sorbet in Lightly Curried Tulip Case (opposite) followed by Loin of Pork Marinated in Coconut Milk with Pineapple (above).

Meringue Basket

Meringues are very easy to make and store extremely well either in the freezer or well wrapped in an airtight container. Small individual meringues are often a godsend for a quickly put-together pud, and if you make a 'basket' you have the basis of a spectacular *finale. Fill it with fresh fruit salad, summer berries, or with the poached spiced peaches and/or apricots on page 125. Fresh whipped double (heavy) cream – flavoured if you like – is the other essential accompaniment. Please don't fill your meringues or 'baskets' until the last minute, though.*

So many people, however, seem to be scared of making meringues and actually say they can't. *The points to remember for consistent success are these:*

1. Older *egg whites are much better than fresher as they contain more acid, and older eggs are even better if they are separated the day before (I find I have a storage jar of egg whites constantly during the summer when I am making mayonnaise and ice cream), as some of the moisture evaporates leaving a more concentrated solution of the albumen.*

2. *It is* essential *that your bowl is spotlessly clean and totally devoid of any grease. Stainless steel, glass and copper are ideal, but unfortunately some of the bowls on electric mixers seem to build up a slightly greasy and textured lining over the months. I invariably rub whatever bowl I am going to use with half a lemon as the acid in this helps to stabilize the mix.*

3. Weigh *out the egg whites rather than assume that one egg white weighs 25 g (1 oz). In fact, if you stockpile your egg whites as mentioned above, you will* have *to weigh them.*

4. *Whatever the egg whites weigh, then you want* twice *that of sugar.*

5. *The sugar – use caster (superfine) – should always be* dry, *and if you have any doubt whatsoever, spread it over a baking sheet and put in a warm oven for 5 minutes. Always pass the sugar through a fine sieve to get rid of any lumps.*

6. *Put the egg whites into your mixing bowl and beat them until they start to form a strong texture and then (and* only *then) start to beat in the sugar a* tablespoon at a time. *If you throw several ounces in at one fell swoop the mixture will fall back and you will never get the same result. I painstakingly add up to two-thirds of the sugar in this manner and then gently (using a long-handled spoon or spatula), fold in the balance.*

7. *Good greaseproof (wax) paper is of prime importance (Bakewell, for*

instance), and please don't economize on this or the meringues will stick and you will have a devil of a job getting them off.

8. *Initially heat your oven up to 180°C/350°F/mark 4 and just before you place your prepared meringues in, turn it down to 110°C/225°F/mark ¼. After an hour, top and bottom the trays and after a further hour, check and repeat the process. You want the meringues to be crisp and dry.*

I make no bones about the fact that this meringue basket is very time-consuming but it is well worth the time and trouble as it does look good and professional. After a couple of guests have hacked a portion out of it, however, it can look a little sad and pathetic, but don't despair, it will taste divine.

**MAKES 1 ROUND BASE
AND 3 RINGS**
110 g (4 oz) egg whites
a pinch of salt
225 g (8 oz/1 cup) caster
   (superfine) sugar, sieved
FINISHING 'PASTE'
50 g (2 oz) egg whites
100 g (4 oz/½ cup) caster sugar

Put the first lot of egg whites and the salt into a clean bowl and follow the method outlined in note 6 above for adding the sugar.

On your greaseproof (wax) paper mark out with pencil four circles of 20 cm (8 inch) in diameter. Lay the paper on baking sheets. Have a large piping bag with plastic nozzle to hand. Fill this with the prepared meringue and pipe one full flat circle, the base of your basket. Pipe a thick band only round the perimeter of the other three pencilled circles: these bands when cooked will be 'stuck' together for the basket sides.

Cook as instructed in note 8 above. Remove from the oven and allow to cool.

Beat up the 'paste' egg whites with the caster sugar. Lay one complete base circle on a plate and put about eight blobs of 'paste' around its edges. On top of this lay your first band, and then repeat pasting and laying on of bands until finished. Return to the oven, having covered the basket totally with foil, and cook for a further 1½ hours. Remove foil and leave for a further 30 minutes.

You can go one stage further and make up *another* small meringue mix. This can be piped into S shapes, cooked off, and then stuck on to the sides of the basket and returned to the oven! This is for extra security and a certain visual nicety – for the basket, please remember, is very fragile.

Overleaf: Beetroot (Beet) and Claret Soup (page 136) followed by Roast Beef (page 136) with roast potatoes and horseradish cream tartlets, plus Junket (page 137) and Shortbread Rounds (page 79).

Beetroot (Beet) and Claret Soup with Yoghurt and Toasted Almonds

Beetroot is a much maligned vegetable. This is a favourite soup of mine and, in my opinion, better than boring borsch!

SERVES 6

100 g (4 oz/½ cup) butter

225 g (8 oz) onions, peeled and finely chopped

900 g (2 lb) cooked beetroots (beet), peeled and evenly chopped

150 ml (¼ pint/⅔ cup) cooking sherry

600 ml (1 pint/2½ cups) chicken stock

600 ml (1 pint/2½ cups) inexpensive claret

grated rind of 1 orange

Melt the butter in a saucepan and sauté the onions until golden. Add the beetroot (beet), sherry, chicken stock, red wine and orange rind. Bring to the boil, then simmer for 30 minutes. Liquidize and pass through a sieve.

The soup may be served hot or cold, but should be topped with a generous sprinkling of toasted flaked almonds and then a dollop of thick yoghurt.

Roast Beef

No matter how religiously you follow this simple recipe, if you haven't bought well hung beef, you are bound to be disappointed with the results. Hanging, despite the fact that it means meat loss, improves both the flavour and texture of meat, and is vitally important with beef particularly. At Miller Howe, the large sirloins of Lakeland beef are often 4 weeks old before they are trimmed and then roasted. They carve ethereally and are full of flavour. The only advice I can give is to find a reliable butcher and to give him plenty of warning of your needs; if he responds, then support him, buying from him regularly!

Go for a well hung sirloin which has tiny particles of fat running through it; these act as an automatic 'baster' while the meat is cooking. To serve six, buy a sirloin on the bone weighing at least 2.25 kg (5 lb). Before you cook it, let it hang around out of fridge and wrappings for over an hour, and then rub a little salt mixed with some curry powder into the fat. This will help you achieve a crisp, brown skin. Sprinkle plain (all-purpose) flour on the base of your roasting tin (baking pan) and then place the seasoned joint, bone side down, with fat/skin towards you. Start the cooking in a preheated oven at 220°C/425°F/mark 7 for the first 15 minutes, and then reduce the temperature to 190°C/375°F/mark 5 for the rest of the cooking time. Roughly speaking, roast for 15 minutes per 450g (1 lb) for rare beef; 20 minutes for medium; and up to 30 minutes for well done meat. (Pleb as I am, I prefer the latter!) Should you be roasting the meat to be served cold, however, it should be cooked to a rare stage as it is much more tender.

Work out your cooking time to allow for 10–15 minutes at the end of cooking: the meat should stand in the warm kitchen to rest when it has come out of the oven, as this allows the juices to settle. It will also be easier to carve.

Meanwhile, you will have roasted your potatoes, made your Yorkshire puddings (use the popover recipe on page 26 – but omit the marmalade!) and prepared your vegetables to cook off at the last moment. For an added touch, make some small pastry cases as on page 141 while the meat is roasting (or in advance, of course, in your well organized weekend way). Fill them with horseradish cream garnished with walnut halves and parsley sprigs.

Junket

This is a fairly unpleasant word to describe a simple and delicious dish, one that has, unfortunately, virtually disappeared from the culinary scene. In my childhood, it was prepared most weeks and served with home-made shortbread (see page 79).

All you require is a small bottle of rennet essence (small because it goes off very quickly if left half full, losing its magic setting power), and 600 ml (1 pint/2½ cups) farm milk. Bring the milk just up to blood heat (37°C/98.6°F) and pour into your pretty serving dish with 1 teaspoon of the rennet essence. Stir for a few minutes and then leave at room temperature to set. Junket will keep in a fridge overnight, but it is much nicer left at room temperature and then served thus too.

Margaret Costa served this dish at her Hampstead home and used to add 15 ml (3 teaspoons) of Camp (extra strong liquid) coffee to the rennet and milk to give a light coffee flavour. I like this a lot, and I grate fresh nutmeg on the top. I often serve this coffee junket in the summer with a bowl of fresh summer fruits in the middle of the table.

Smoked Salmon in Walnut Spinach Nest with Poached Egg and Hollandaise

This is a new favourite of mine as I do like the idea of mixing spinach with good smoked salmon – even if purists will raise their eyes to heaven and say, 'There goes that mad Tovey again'! But more important still, everything apart from the hollandaise can be prepared the day before: make up individual dishes if you have sufficient storage space, and they will come to no harm overnight covered with clingfilm (plastic wrap) in the fridge. (To pad it out you can, if you like, put a round baked bread croûton on the base of the dish under the spinach nest.)

SERVES 6

100 g (4 oz) fresh spinach leaves, stalks removed

a touch of good walnut oil

175 g (6 oz) good smoked salmon, cut into thin slices

6 soft poached eggs (see page 20)

HOLLANDAISE

3 egg yolks

a pinch of salt

1 teaspoon caster (superfine) sugar

15 ml (1 tablespoon) each of white wine vinegar and fresh lemon juice, heated together

175 g (6 oz/$\frac{3}{4}$ cup) butter, melted

Wipe the spinach leaves clean with a damp cloth, and then roll them up like a cigar. Very thinly slice with a sharp knife. Mix the spinach shreds with walnut oil, then divide between six plates. Push the shreds out from the centre to make a bird's nest shape. Roll up the smoked salmon like a scarf, and wind this around the inside of the spinach nest. Place the poached egg in the middle. Leave in the fridge overnight, covered with clingfilm (plastic wrap).

Make the hollandaise sauce at the last minute. Place the egg yolks in a liquidizer or food processor with the salt and sugar and blend well. Slowly pour on the heated wine vinegar and lemon juice – the machine running at top speed – then, when this has been taken up by the egg yolks, dribble in the heated butter little by little. It is important that you take care, because if you pour the butter in too quickly, or when it's too cool, your sauce will be extremely thin like evaporated milk. You are looking for something more like condensed milk. Coat the egg and salmon using a large tablespoon and serve at once.

Roast Guinea Fowl

Use guinea fowl weighing approximately 900 g (2 lb) each. They lack that free-range gamey flavour but a distinct improvement is made by marinating the birds.

SERVES 6

3 guinea fowl

sea salt and freshly ground black
  pepper

MARINADE

180 ml (12 tablespoons) red wine

15 ml (1 tablespoon) red wine
  vinegar

100 g (4 oz) onions, peeled and
  coarsely chopped

1 garlic clove, peeled and
  crushed

6 black peppercorns

6 juniper berries

2 bay leaves

*P*lace all the marinade ingredients in a saucepan and bring to boiling point. Leave to cool a little.

Wipe the guinea fowl dry and coat with a generous sprinkling of sea salt and freshly ground black pepper. Place each bird in a plastic bag and divide the marinade evenly between the bags. Close with a twist-tie. Place the bags in a roasting tin (baking pan) and leave in the fridge. Give them a turn twice daily for up to 5–6 days.

When you want to cook, remove the birds from the plastic bags and simply put them back into the roasting tin with the marinade. Cook in a preheated oven at 220°C/425°F/mark 7 for $1\frac{1}{4}$ hours, basting occasionally.

Cut each bird in half lengthways and serve with either a simple bread sauce or a fruit purée. The latter are combinations of 450 g (1 lb) fruit of choice with an appropriate flavouring, simmered with 25 g (1 oz/2 tablespoons) butter and 75 g (3 oz/$\frac{1}{2}$ cup) finely chopped onions until soft, then liquidized and sieved. Good purées would be gooseberries and elderflowers, rhubarb and ginger, apple and Calvados or sage.

Syllabub

This makes a delicious change for the topping of a trifle, but can also be put into small glass custard cups and served as a sweet. It can also be used as the filling for a sponge cake, perhaps mixed with some chopped wine jelly (see next page).

150 ml ($\frac{1}{4}$ pint/$\frac{2}{3}$ cup) dry white
  wine

juice and finely grated rind of 1
  lemon

300 ml ($\frac{1}{2}$ pint/$1\frac{1}{4}$ cups) double
  (heavy) cream

2 tablespoons caster (superfine)
  sugar

*M*ix the wine and lemon juice and rind together and leave, covered, in the fridge overnight.

The next day, shortly before you wish to serve, beat the cream to the peak stage with the caster sugar. Strain the wine and lemon juice (discard the rind) and add to the beaten cream, a little at a time. continually beating.

Simple Wine Jelly

My Port and Claret Jelly is very popular at Miller Howe, but it's so boozy, and I personally prefer this extremely simple jelly, made with wine. Use dry, medium or sweet according to taste and pocket. It is such a 'clean' finish to a meal, and can be 'upgraded' by adding fresh seasonal berries before setting. (One of the finest puddings I have had in all my hundreds of thousands of miles' flying was simply this on a British Airways flight. It had been made in a ramekin and when turned out hardly wobbled, was crystal clear and was the perfect ending to a delicious lunch.)

600 ml (1 pint/2½ cups) wine of
   choice
30 ml (2 tablespoons) caster
   (superfine) sugar (optional)
15 g (½ oz) powdered gelatine
fruit of choice (optional)

Measure the wine out into a saucepan, add the sugar if you want, and bring to a simmer. Sprinkle on the gelatine. It is essential that you now continually stir for about 5 minutes in a gentle fashion to make sure all the gelatine dissolves (otherwise it will immediately sink to the base of the pan and stick). When the liquid is cooling, pass through a fine sieve into six glasses, ramekins or cups (or, of course, into a large glass bowl). Add the fruit if you like and leave to set.

Instead of dividing between individual containers, you could pour the liquid jelly on to a plastic tray to set. Thereafter, you can cut or chop the sheet of jelly up to serve with syllabub (previous page) as the filling in a sponge cake.

Tuna and Cheese Pastry Tartlets

The pastry is very easy to make and extremely short in texture, resulting in a delicious tartlet. One per person is ideal for a starter, but two can be served for a main course with some mashed potatoes. The pastry will also be enough for three open 20 cm (8 inch) flans, or the large lidded pie on page 60.

Other fillings throughout the book could be used instead of the tuna one below – the cheese, onion and chutney on page 49, for instance.

MAKES 18 TARTLETS

CHEESE PASTRY
450 g (1 lb/3 cups) strong plain (hard all-purpose) flour
225 g (8 oz) strong Cheddar cheese, finely grated
225 g (8 oz/1 cup) hard butter, roughly grated
a pinch of salt
a touch of paprika or curry powder (optional)

FILLING
50 g (2 oz/4 tablespoons) butter
100 g (4 oz) onions, peeled and finely chopped
450 g (1 lb) tuna canned in oil, drained and flaked
olive oil

*B*ring all the pastry ingredients together in your food mixer on a slow speed, using the beater. Use your hands to mould it into two balls, one two-thirds, and one one-third. Wrap each in clingfilm (plastic wrap) and leave to chill. Bring out and when starting to become pliable (which depends on the heat of your kitchen), roll the larger ball of pastry out and cut into eighteen 7.5 cm (3 inch) circles. Place in tartlet tins (pans) and press gently around the sides. Put in the fridge to chill again while you preheat the oven to 190°C/375°F/mark 5. Line the pastry bases with foil and fill with dried peas or baking beans. Bake blind for 15 minutes, then cool.

Meanwhile, roll out the remaining ball of pastry to make the lids. Cut these smaller in diameter, about 6.25 cm (2½ inch). Any surplus pastry may be re-rolled and used to decorate the lids after they are put in place.

To make the filling, melt the butter, and cook the onion until golden. Mix with the tuna and spoon out into the cold pastry cases. Put 5 ml (1 teaspoon) of oil on top before you fit on the lids – use a little water to make them stick – and then bake for a further 20 minutes at a reduced temperature – 160°C/325°F/mark 3. Leave out of the oven for 5 minutes, then turn out and serve by themselves or with a cream sauce. (I once had some savoury quiche custard left over, so I divided it between six dishes to make a thin coating, baked this quickly in a hot oven, and served the tartlets on top with the cream sauce.)

Overleaf: Tuna and Cheese Pastry Tartlets (above) followed by Leg of Lamb Stuffed with Preserved Ginger, Garlic and Rosemary (page 144), and Coeurs à la Crème (page 145) with raspberries.

Leg of Lamb Studded with Preserved Ginger, Garlic and Rosemary with Two Sauces

At Miller Howe we always buy hogs so they are at least 15 months when killed. The carcasses are then hung, on the hoof, for 3 weeks before butchering. This makes the meat very tasty, and while garlic and rosemary are traditional flavourings, the ginger adds a hint of further sweetness.

SERVES 6

1 leg of lamb

6–7 fat garlic cloves, peeled and
  halved

slivers of preserved (candied)
  ginger

sprigs of rosemary

60 ml (4 tablespoons) each of
  runny honey and soy sauce

**PINEAPPLE AND MINT
  SAUCE**

12 sprigs fresh mint

30 ml (2 tablespoons) white wine
  vinegar

10 ml (2 teaspoons) caster
  (superfine) sugar

75 ml (5 tablespoons) water or
  dry white wine

3 slices fresh pineapple, cored
  and very finely chopped

**RED (BELL) PEPPER
  CREAM SAUCE**

600 ml (1 pint/2½ cups) double
  (heavy) cream, reduced by half

50 g (2 oz/4 tablespoons) butter

100 g (4 oz) onions, peeled and
  coarsely sliced

2 red (bell) peppers, seeded and
  cut into chunks

60 ml (4 tablespoons) white wine

Make 12–14 slits in the skin of the leg, and insert a half clove of garlic, a sliver of preserved ginger and a sprig of rosemary in each. Bring the runny honey and soy sauce to the boil and then pour over the leg, which should be in a roasting tin (baking pan). Cover with clingfilm (plastic wrap) and leave for 4 days, turning morning and evening.

When you wish to cook the leg, preheat the oven to 200°C/400°F/mark 6, paint the leg finally with the marinade, and put in the oven. Baste the leg every 20 minutes throughout its cooking time of $1\frac{1}{2}$–$1\frac{3}{4}$ hours. The meat is then free from blood and extremely tasty.

Meanwhile make the sauces. Mix the ingredients for the pineapple and mint sauce together and place in a bowl or dish on the table. (This makes rather a good edible gift too!) While the cream is reducing for the red (bell) pepper sauce, melt the butter and cook the onions until golden. Add the prepared peppers and wine, and simmer away for 30–40 minutes until the peppers are fairly soft. Transfer all to your liquidizer, blend and then pass through a coarse sieve. Add this liquid to the reduced cream.

Serve the slices of lamb on top of the red pepper cream sauce, passing the pineapple and mint sauce separately.

Coeurs à la Crème

Traditionally these should be made, obviously, in the special heart-shaped dishes with holes which allow the whey to drain away. If you do not wish to invest in these, however, a very large wire strainer can be used: line it with muslin and leave over a large bowl to drip. Serve in dollops on individual plates.

SERVES 6

300 ml ($\frac{1}{2}$ pint/1$\frac{1}{4}$ cups) double (heavy) cream

a pinch of salt

50 g (2 oz/$\frac{1}{3}$ cup) caster (superfine) sugar

225 g (8 oz/1 cup) full-fat cream cheese (the richest you can obtain)

2 egg whites

Beat the cream in a large bowl with the salt and sugar until it holds its shape. Pass the cream cheese through a fine plastic sieve into the whipped cream and fold together. In another bowl, using very clean beaters, beat the egg whites until really stiff.

Fold the stiff egg whites gently into the cheese and cream mixture, making sure you have just finished beating them immediately prior to incorporating with the other ingredients. Meanwhile, lightly oil six heart dishes and line them with plenty of muslin, allowing this to come up and slightly over the sides; or use a double thickness of muslin in a large sieve. Divide the mixture between the six dishes, lightly press down and leave on a cooling tray over a baking tray or tin (pan) to catch the whey. Put in a cool place.

Most recipes for this dish say that you can eat or use after 24 hours and you can, of course. But it's much tastier, with a certain bite, if you leave for 72 hours! For serving, I lift the cream hearts out of the dishes and remove the muslin (wash it, save it and use it again). I wash the dishes themselves, and place in them summer fruits such as redcurrants, raspberries, blueberries, loganberries etc, and serve these alongside the cream heart, on a pretty plate.

EDIBLE GIFTS

You have already taken good care of your guests over the weekend: you have enjoyed their company, the getting up-to-date with news, the parlour games, the walks, etc. But to give them just a little parting gift as they go out to their cars (a few pounds heavier in body, perhaps, but so much lighter spiritually) will set the seal on your entertaining!

I don't just give little presents when entertaining at home. When giving private dinner parties in restaurants I have often arranged for the ladies to be presented as they are leaving with the simplest of hedgerow flowers made up lovingly into small bunches wrapped in old doyleys, and then brought together with kitchen foil and tied with a pretty ribbon. They can be plonked straight into a vase at home and be a reminder of that happy evening for several days.

The *size* of the gift doesn't matter, it's the thought that counts, remember. You don't have to give a jam or chutney in a pound quantity: save little paste or make-up jars, or those smaller glass marmalade screw-top pots, and fill them with a chutney, lemon curd, or a French dressing or sauce that a guest has particularly liked (see pages 93 and 144). Cut out some pretty material in circles with pinking shears and attach to the top of the jar with an elastic band. Plastic containers can be bought and filled with some shortbread biscuits or the fudge – or wrap up in cellophane and tie with a ribbon bow.

If you have a flourishing herb garden, nothing could be nicer for the guests who have enjoyed your lavish weekend hospitality than to go away with a positive memento of your cleverness! This could be in the form of a little container of dried herbs, a single or mixed bunch of dried herbs, or a bottle of herb oil or vinegar. Home-dried herbs, if done properly, contribute wonderfully to all cookery (although nothing is better than fresh). Oils and vinegars are essential, but when they are given the additional flavour of herbs, they are transformed into something very much more special. They are all fun to do, and very easy indeed.

Dried Herbs

Harvest them just before the flowers form, on a dry morning. Handle them carefully as bruising will release the volatile oils which give them their flavour. The best herbs for drying are lovage, marjoram, mint, sage, savory, oregano, lemon balm, borage and bergamot flowers, bay, rosemary and thyme.

Separate into sprigs and hang in bunches in a dry, airy, shady room – from a washing line, perhaps, if you're doing a lot. Or place leaves and sprigs in a single layer on a muslin-covered rack, cover with more muslin, and leave in the same dry, airy and shady room. Drying can take from 2–7 days.

Fleshier herbs like sage, mint and lovage can be put on trays in the oven at its lowest possible setting. Prop the door slightly open with something like a wooden spoon handle. They should be dried in about an hour.

Crumble leaves off stalks to put in an attractive little container, or tie bunches together with pretty ribbon.

Herb Vinegars

Flavoured vinegars were once much more widely used and have recently come back into fashion with raspberry and tarragon vinegars available commercially. However, it is much nicer to make them at home.

Use cider or wine vinegars which will not mask the delicate flavours of the herbs. One exception is horseradish vinegar which should be made with malt (and which only takes about 1 week for its pungency to be conveyed). Experiment with various vinegars – red for garlic, white for tarragon or basil, cider for mint, say. Horseradish vinegar would be good with a beef salad dressing, or you could mix it with some dry English mustard powder; dill vinegar would be ideal for a cucumber salad, and your own home-made tarragon vinegar would be wonderful for a classic béarnaise sauce.

**a good 45 ml (3 tablespoons)
  fresh herbs**
900 ml (1½ pints/3¾ cups) vinegar

Put the herbs, slightly bruised, into a large jar and cover with vinegar. Seal with cork or plastic (never metal), and leave in a dark place for at least 10 days. Shake the jar occasionally as with herb oil. Strain, if you like, and repeat the process as with herb oil. Strain into bottles, add a fresh herb sprig, label and date.

Herb Oils

Use a base oil which has the blandest, least pronounced flavour – sunflower, safflower, corn (maize), grapeseed and peanut are all suitable.

The herbs to use depend on what you've got, of course. A basil oil would be lovely with a tomato salad; fennel would complement fish; a tarragon oil mayonnaise would enliven cold chicken; and rosemary oil would be ideal for brushing over lamb to be grilled or barbecued.

**a good 60 ml (4 tablespoons)
   fresh herbs**
600 ml (1 pint/2½ cups) oil

Wash the herbs well and pat them dry. Crush them a little, put them into an appropriately sized bottle, and cover with the oil. Put the oil in a sunny place and agitate the bottle a couple of times a day. Leave for at least 14 days before using.

You could strain away the first lot of herbs after about 10 days and repeat the process with *fresh* bruised herbs to make the flavour stronger. Sprinkle a little oil on your hand; it should be really pungent.

As a final and decorative touch, you could add a sprig of the fresh herb to the strained oil. Label carefully with ingredients and date.

Cheese and Herb Pâté

I've given the recipe for this – and for the mushroom pâté opposite – in every book I've had published, and my only excuse is that I use them in my cooking so often, that I couldn't possibly put together any collection of recipes without them! Both are so useful in so many ways – but they also make very good edible gifts, packed into nice little jars (they need to be refrigerated).

150 g (5 oz/⅔ cup) butter
**450 g (1 lb/2 cups) full fat cream
   cheese**
**3 garlic cloves, crushed with a
   little salt**
**15 ml (1 tablespoon) each of
   finely chopped chervil, parsley
   or chives (or any other fresh
   herbs to hand)**

Melt the butter very slowly in a saucepan while, using an electric hand-held whisk, you mix the other ingredients together in a large bowl. Make sure the herbs are evenly distributed.

When the butter has cooled a little, pour it very slowly into the cream cheese mixture. Fold in carefully – it could curdle – and when all has been absorbed, spoon the pâté into your chosen container or containers. Leave to cool, then store in the fridge.

Mushroom Pâté

A must for every freezer and every serious cook as it has endless uses.

100 g (4 oz/½ cup) butter
225 g (8 oz) onions, peeled and
    minced (ground)
900 g (2 lb) mushrooms, trimmed
    and minced (ground)
a generous pinch of sea salt
freshly ground black pepper
600 ml (1 pint/2½ cups) red wine

Melt the butter gently in a large pan, add the onions, and simmer for about 10 minutes. Add the mushrooms, salt and pepper, and stir well before adding the red wine. Leave to bubble over a very low heat for about 2–3 hours, during which time the red wine will gradually evaporate, leaving the mixture fairly dry. Remove from the heat, leave to get cold, then pot as appropriate and chill.

Tomato Chutney

Tomatoes that are 'over the hill' are best for this recipe (and so are economical if bought cannily from the local market). Drain well, after skinning, seeding and quartering, on layers of kitchen paper towels, to dry them.

MAKES ABOUT 1.8 kg (4 lb)
1 tablespoon olive oil
25 g (1 oz/2 tablespoons) butter
225 g (8 oz) onions, peeled and
    finely chopped
2.7 kg (6 lb) ripe tomatoes,
    skinned, seeded and quartered
300 ml (½ pint/1¼ cups) distilled
    white vinegar
10 ml (2 teaspoons) sea salt
a good pinch each of mixed spice
    and cayenne (ground red)
    pepper
50 g (2 oz/⅓ cup) allspice berries
    securely tied in a muslin bag
350 g (12 oz/1¾ cups) demerara
    (brown) sugar

Heat the oil in a frying pan (skillet), then add the butter and melt. Sauté the onion until golden, then remove from the pan and drain on kitchen paper towels. Return the onions to a clean saucepan and add the tomatoes. Leave to simmer until you have a dryish paste: it could take 10 minutes or 20 or (heaven forbid!) a little longer. Add half the vinegar with the salt, mixed spice, cayenne (ground red) pepper and bag of allspice berries. Simmer for a further 30 minutes, when the mixture should once again be thick.

Meanwhile put the remaining vinegar in another saucepan with the sugar and cook until all the sugar has dissolved. Add this to the dry tomato mixture and cook for a further 1–1½ hours when it will be fairly thick.

Fill your jars with boiling water, empty and dry, then spoon in the chutney. Cover and seal.

Overleaf: a selection of home-made chutneys and jellies, with 'bouquets' of home-grown herbs: ideal edible gifts for your parting guests.

Curried Apricot Chutney

I always buy some of this from farm stalls when I am out in the Cape. It goes so well with the flavoursome Karoo lamb dishes they serve there, and with cold meats.

MAKES ABOUT 1.8 kg (4 lb)
675 g (1½ lb) dried apricots
90 ml (6 tablespoons) cooking
   brandy
450 g (1 lb) onions, peeled and
   roughly chopped
600 ml (1 pint/2½ cups) malt
   vinegar
10 ml (2 teaspoons) salt
5 ml (1 teaspoon) turmeric
30 ml (2 tablespoons) curry
   powder
15 ml (1 tablespoon) English
   (dry) mustard powder
450 g (1 lb/2⅓ cups) soft brown
   sugar
225 g (8 oz/1⅓ cups) sultanas
   (white raisins)

Soak the dried apricots overnight in the cooking brandy. The next day mince (grind) them with the onions. I find I can't do this successfully in a food processor as I either go just that little bit too far and end up with mush, or not far enough and have big lumps!

Put into a saucepan along with half the malt vinegar, the salt, turmeric, curry powder and mustard, and simmer for 30 minutes until the mixture is soft.

In another saucepan dissolve the sugar in the remaining vinegar, then add to the pan of apricots. Simmer for 1–2 hours until the mixture is quite thick. Fold in the sultanas (white raisins), spoon into sterile jars and seal.

Date Chutney

My good friend Margaret Costa introduced me to this chutney, and I feel no remorse in quoting it again – it's so delicious as an accompaniment for high teas.

MAKES ABOUT 1.4 kg (3 lb)
900 g (2 lb) stoned dates
450 g (1 lb) onions, peeled and
   roughly chopped
600 ml (1 pint/2½ cups) malt
   vinegar
50 g (2 oz/6 tablespoons) sea salt
5 ml (1 teaspoon) ground ginger
75 g (3 oz/½ cup) allspice berries,
   securely tied in a muslin bag
450 g (1 lb/2¼ cups) soft brown
   sugar

Put the dates and onions through a mincer (grinder). Bring a third of the vinegar to simmering point in a large saucepan then add the salt, ginger, the allspice bag, and the minced (ground) dates and onions. Simmer over low heat until thick.

Meanwhile dissolve the sugar in the remainder of the vinegar and then add to the thickened mixture in the pan. Simmer again until thick, then remove the allspice bag. When cool, pour into washed, sterile jars, and seal.

Pickled Onions

Nothing could be nicer than home-pickled onions in old-fashioned jars on the high-tea table – delicious with pies, cold meats and a variety of other things.

900 g (2 lb) button (pearl) or pickling onions
30 ml (2 tablespoons) kitchen salt
600 ml (1 pint/2½ cups) malt vinegar
15 g (½ oz/1½ tablespoons) sea salt
15 g (½ oz/1½ tablespoons) pickling spice
6 cloves
10 g (¼ oz/1 tablespoon) black peppercorns
50 g (2 oz/3 tablespoons) demerara (brown) sugar

To peel the onions quickly, top and tail them carefully, then immerse in boiling water. Leave to soak for 4 minutes. Drain and slip the skins off as quickly as possible. Spread the peeled onions out on a large tray, sprinkle them generously with kitchen salt, and leave overnight.

The next day, rinse the onions well, getting rid of all the salt, and pat dry thoroughly with kitchen paper. Mix the remaining ingredients together in a large saucepan and boil for 10 minutes. Add the onions and bring the mixture back to the boil. Remove immediately from the heat, take out the onions, and pack them into washed, sterilized jars. Reheat the vinegar mixture and pour over the onions in the jars. Leave to become cold, then cover.

Leave for at least 4 weeks before sampling!

Onion and Red (Bell) Pepper Marmalade

You won't have much of this left after all the cooking, but it is well worth the trouble as it is superb with so many dishes (see pages 57 and 112, for instance).

MAKES ABOUT 350 g (12 oz)
60 ml (4 tablespoons) olive oil
900 g (2 lb) onions, peeled and very finely sliced
3 red (bell) peppers, seeded then sliced very thinly indeed
120 ml (8 tablespoons) demerara (brown) sugar
90 ml (6 tablespoons) sherry vinegar

Warm the oil through in a saucepan, add the finely sliced onions and peppers, and cook, stirring constantly, until they soak up the oil. Add the sugar and leave to simmer for 1½ hours. You will have to stir with a wooden spoon from time to time to make sure they don't 'catch' on the bottom of the pan.

Add the sherry vinegar, 2 tablespoons at a time, and stir quite vigorously so that it is evenly distributed. Cook for a further 30–45 minutes. The mixture should be slightly oily.

Sweet and Sour Jellies

My main failing in the 'taste' department is that I have a rather sweet tooth, so beware — these jellies may be too sweet for you.

I use commercial packet jellies (Jell-O), but instead of using the recommended 600 ml (1 pint/2½ cups) water, I use 150 ml (¼ pint/⅔ cup) plus 30 ml (2 tablespoons) of white wine vinegar, and make this up to 600 ml (1 pint/2½ cups) with boiling water. Have some sterilized jars to hand on a tray which will fit into your fridge, and when the basic jelly is made and melted, quarter-fill the jars with the appropriate jelly and a quarter of the appropriate 'filling'. Put into the fridge to set and then you repeat the process three or so more times so that you have jelly with evenly distributed 'filling'. They look pretty, are ideal for take-away edible gifts and are delicious with cold meats or, occasionally, curries.

Lime Jelly

Add grated courgettes (zucchini) well squeezed in a teatowel, or some whole gooseberries.

Redcurrant Jelly

Add fresh redcurrants, of course, or wild Alpine strawberries or raspberries.

Blackcurrant Jelly

Add fresh blackcurrants, blackberries or blueberries.

Lemon Jelly

Add grated celeriac (celery root) or celery with finely sliced radishes and a little grated horseradish.

Home-made Lemon Curd

This is nice spooned into small jars and given to guests to take home. It could also play its part throughout the weekend though: spread on toast or bread at breakfast and tea, or as a filling for tartlets or sponge cakes.

MAKES ABOUT 450 g (1 lb)
110 g (4 oz/½ cup) unsalted butter
225 g (8 oz/1¼ cups) caster
  (superfine) sugar
juice and finely grated rind of 2
  lemons
4 egg yolks

Place a mixing bowl over a saucepan of gently simmering water. Place all the ingredients in the bowl and beat together. Stir continuously with a wooden spoon over the same gentle heat until the mixture starts to thicken — mine usually takes about 45–50 minutes. Do not overcook, though, as it will set and thicken further as it cools. Pour into clean, sterile pots and cover.

Coconut Cream Fudge

The awful thing about this is that I often have to double the recipe. When it comes to the time that the fudge is given to departing guests, I have eaten most of it myself...

MAKES OVER 450 g (1 lb)

450 g (1 lb/2¼ cups) granulated sugar

150 ml (¼ pint/⅔ cup) coconut milk

15 ml (1 tablespoon) golden syrup

150 ml (¼ pint/⅔ cup) double (heavy) cream

25 g (1 oz/2 tablespoons) butter

75 g (3 oz/1 cup) desiccated (shredded) coconut, toasted

Grease a 17.5 cm (7 inch) shallow square baking tin (pan) well with extra butter.

Put the sugar and coconut milk in a large thick-bottomed saucepan and cook, stirring continually, over a low heat until the sugar has dissolved. Beat in the golden syrup and turn up the heat.

It is *essential* that you have a sugar thermometer as you must now bring the mixture to the boil *without stirring*. When the thermometer reaches 110°C/230°F/ (about 10 minutes), add half the cream and continue to boil – this time stirring occasionally – until the temperature reaches 114°C/238°F (about a further 5 minutes). Then put in the balance of the cream and boil further – stirring occasionally again – until it reaches the magic 115°C/240°F (a further 2 minutes). Remove from the heat and submerge the bottom half of the saucepan in very cold water to stop the mixture cooking further.

Beat in the butter along with the coconut. Allow to cool then stir with a wooden spoon quite vigorously and pour into the prepared tin. When it is starting to set, mark the fudge into squares (whatever size you want), and leave until it cools completely. Turn it out of the tin, break into the squares, and put in bags. Or eat, of course...

Coffee Cream Fudge

This can be made, following the recipe as above, but at the end you add 2 teaspoons Camp (extra strong liquid) coffee instead of the coconut. You could also add some sultanas (white raisins) or chopped pecan nuts.

INDEX

The **bold** numerals indicate actual recipes.

Afternoon teas 64–83
Apricots: Poached Spiced Peaches
    and Apricots **125**
    Curried Apricot Chutney **152**
Almonds 124, 136
Apples: Apple and Date Batter
    Ginger Slice **73**, 74–5
    Apple, Lime, Grape and
        Mushroom Salad **96**
    Calvados Apple Duck Liver Pâté
        114–15, **117**
    Cottage Cheese with Grapes, Red
        (bell) Pepper and Apple Salad
        98
    Curried Stuffed Apples **28**
    Pork with Sage, Onion and Apple
        Purée (pizza) **53**
    purée 53
    Radish, Apple and Celeriac (celery
        root) Salad **98**
Aubergine (eggplant) 61

Bacon: in baked potatoes 108
    Bacon Chops in Wine with
        Curried Stuffed Apples **28**, 29,
        30–1
    Broad Beans with Bacon Bits
        (salad) **97**
    Cheese, Bacon and Olive Pizza **53**
    Duck Liver with Bacon **113**
    in pizzas 53
    in quiches 57
    in salads 93, 94–5
    in savoury custards 21
    Watercress, Orange and Walnut
        with Bacon Bits (salad) **98**
Baked Trout in Coriander Butter
    45, 61, 62–3
Barbecues 32–63
Basil: Quick Tomato and Basil Soup
    35
Batter, beer 88
Beans: Broad Beans with Bacon Bits
    (salad) **97**
    French Bean and New Potato
        Salad with Mustard Dressing
        97
    red kidney beans 99
    runner beans 105
Beef: Herbed Beef Guinness
    Casserole **119**
    Macaroni Beef Savoury **118**
    Picnic Meat Pie **60**
    Plaited Pastry Loaf **116**
    in profiteroles 55
    Roast Beef 134–5, **136–7**
    Savoury Beef Topped with Baked
        Potato Circles **26**
    Savoury Mince Turnover **49**

Beef Tomatoes Filled with Peas **105**
Beer-Battered Fish with Chips
    (French Fries) **88**
Beetroot (beet) and Claret Soup with
    Yoghurt and Toasted Almonds
    134–5, **136**
Bell Pepper: *See* Peppers
Blackcurrant Jelly **154**
Boiled Loaf 57, 58–9, 66–7, 68, **69**
Boned Stuffed Quail 34, **44**, 61,
    62–3
Brandy: Passionate Figs with
    Brandy **14**
Braised Ham Steak with Pineapple
    and Herb Topping and Baked
    Egg 14, **29**
Breads: Boiled Loaf 58–9, **69**
    Mini Wheatmeal Loaves 38–9,
        69, 94–5
    in sandwiches 65, 68, 84, 85, 87,
        109
Breadcrumbs, savoury **24**, 37, 45,
    113, 121
Breakfasts and Brunches 9–31
Breast of Chicken with Coconut
    Milk **120–1**
Broccoli: in quiches 57
Buck's Fizz **12**
Butter: Coriander butter 45, 61
    flavoured 68, 73

Cakes: 65, 66–7, 68, 70–1
    Apple and Date Batter Ginger
        Slice **73**, 74–5
    Fairy (cup) Cakes **72–3**, 74–5
    Orange Wedge Cake 66–7, **76**
Pecan, Pineapple, Ginger and
    Hazelnut Frangipane **77**
Sponges 71, **72–3**
Teacakes **86**
Calvados Apple Duck Liver Pâté
    114–15, **117**
Carrot: in baked potatoes 109
    purée 112–13
    in vegetable casserole 121
Casseroles: Bacon Chops in Wine **28**
    Braised Ham Steak **29**
    Breast of Chicken with Coconut
        Milk **120–1**
    Chilled Jellied Poussin (Rock
        Cornish hen) **41**
    Herbed Beef Guinness Casserole
        119
    Lamb Cutlets (rib lamb chops) in
        Orange and Ginger with
        Pineapple **120**
    Savoury Vegetable Casserole **121**
Cauliflower: Cauliflower Cheese on

Onion and Red (bell) Pepper
    Marmalade 32, **112**, 121, 127
    in quiches 57
Celeriac (celery root): in crudités 36
    Radish, Apple and Celeriac Salad
        98
    in vegetable casserole 121
Celery: in baked potatoes 108
    in crudités 36
    in dips 37
Celery Root: *See* Celeriac
Cereals 14, 16
Cheese: in baked potatoes 108
    Cheese, Onion and Chutney
        Turnover **49**
Cheese Pastry 32, 60, 85, **141**
    Cheese Sauce **112**, 121
    Coeurs à la Crème **142–3**, 145
    Cottage Cheese with Grapes, Red
        (bell) Pepper and Apple (salad)
        94–5, **98**
    in dips 37
    Fried Ham and Cheese Sandwich
        109
    in pizzas 53
    in quiches 57
    in salads 93, 94–5, 99
    in sandwiches 87
    Savoury Cheese Balls **40**
    Tuna and Cheese Pastry Tartlets
        78–9, 142–3
Cheese and Herb Pâté 40, 68, 99,
    148
Cherries: 46–7, 48, **120–1**
    Tongue and Cherry Turnover **49**
Chicken: in baked potatoes 108–9
    Breast of Chicken with Coconut
        Milk **120–1**
    Chicken, Mushroom and
        Sweetcorn (corn on the cob)
        Turnover **49**
    Chilled Jellied Poussin (Rock
        Cornish hen) **41**
    livers 21
    in profiteroles 55
    in quail stuffing 44
    in sandwiches 87, 109
    Savoury Chicken Drumsticks in
        Yoghurt with Cornflakes **45**
    stock **104–5**, 121
Chilled Jellied Poussin (Rock
    Cornish hen) **41**
Chips (French Fries) **88**
Chive, Egg and Sour Cream Salad
    96
Chocolate: in 'Cowboy' Coffee 49
    Shortbread Chocolate
        Marshmallow Tartlets **80**, 81–3
Choux pastry 54

INDEX

Chutney: 26, 60, 85, 89, 90–1, 108–9
  Cheese, Chutney and Onion Turnover 49
  Curried Apricot Chutney 152
  Curried Vegetable and Chutney Plaited Pastry Loaf 117
  Date Chutney 152
  Onion and Red (bell) Pepper Marmalade 153
  Pickled Onions 153
Claret: Beetroot (beet) and Claret Soup 136
Coconut: Breast of Chicken with Coconut Milk 120–1
  Coconut Cream Fudge 155
  Loin of Pork Marinated in Coconut Milk 129, 130–1
Coeurs à la Crème 142–3, 145
Coffee: 'Cowboy' Coffee 33, 48, 49
  Coffee Cream Fudge 155
  Coffee Cream Sauce 129, 130–1
Cold Toasted Sandwiches 87
Coriander: Coriander Butter 45, 61
  Savoury Lamb with Coriander (pizza) 53
Corn on the Cob see Sweetcorn
Cornflakes 45
Courgettes (zucchini): Courgettes in Orange Juice Topped with Sour Cream and Mint (salad) 96
  in fish cakes 24
  in quiches 57
  in vegetables kebabs 60–1
  White Fish with Red (bell) Pepper, Grated Courgettes and Lime (fish cake) 24
Crab Fish Cakes with Sweetcorn (corn on the cob) 24
Cream: Coeurs à la Crème 145
  flavoured 73
  horseradish 13, 25, 37, 98, 109, 137
  to reduce 27, 54–5
Cream, sour: in salads 96, 98
  as topping 20, 25
Croûtons 17, 27, 35, 138
Crudités 33, 36–7
Curried Apricot Chutney 152
Curried Drop Scones with Smoked Trout, Horseradish Cream and Keta 13, 18–19, 25
Curried Leftover Vegetable Soups 57, 58–9, 101
Custard: savoury 21, 56, 61
  Sweet 61

Date: Apple and Date Batter Ginger Slice 73, 74–5
Date Chutney 152
Dill: Salmon, Fennel and Dill Fish Cakes 25
Dinners 126–145
Dips 36–7
Duck: in baked potatoes 108

Calvados Apple Duck Liver Pâté 114–15, 117
Duck Liver in Bacon Served with Redcurrant, Mustard and Orange Sauce 113

Edible Gifts 146–155
Eggs: baked 29, 86
  Egg, Chive and Sour Cream Salad 96
  Poached 20, 84, 138
  Salmon, Egg, Rice and Pea Plaited Pastry Loaf 116
  Scrambled 17, 84, 86

Fairy (cup) Cakes 72–3, 74–5
Fennel: Salmon, Fennel and Dill Fish Cake 25
  Smoked Salmon, Waterchestnut and Fennel Pizza 53
Figs: Passionate Figs with Brandy 14
Fish: 17, 21, 48, 53, 55, 57, 68, 109, 116–17
  Baked Trout in Coriander Butter 45
  Beer-Battered Fish with Chips (French Fries) 88
  Curried Drop Scones with Smoked Trout 25
  Fish Cakes 24–5
  Smoked Haddock Chowder 86
  Smoked Salmon in Walnut Spinach Nest 138
  Tuna and Cheese Pastry Tartlets 141
Fish Cakes: 21, 22–3, 24–5
  Crab with Sweetcorn (corn on the cob) 24
  Salmon, Fennel and Dill 25
  Tuna, Pea and Onion 25
  White Fish with Red (bell) Pepper, Grated Courgettes (zucchini) and Lime 24
Frangipane: Pecan, Pineapple, Ginger and Hazelnut 77, 82–3
French Dressing 85, 92, 93, 94, 146
French Fries: See Chips
Fried Ham and Cheese Sandwich 109
Fudge 155

Garlic: Leg of Lamb Studded with Preserved Ginger, Garlic and Rosemary 142–3, 144
  in salads 92
Ginger: Apple and Date Batter Ginger Slice 73
  Lamb Cutlets (rib lamb chops) in Orange and Ginger with Pineapple 120
  Leg of Lamb Studded with Preserved Ginger, Garlic and Rosemary 142–3, 144
  Pecan, Pineapple, Ginger and

Hazelnut Frangipane 77, 82–3
Ginger Beer: Rhubarb Cooked in Ginger Beer 16
Gooseberries 55, 79
Grapes 44, 93
  Apple, Lime, Grape and Mushroom Salad 96
  Cottage Cheese with Grapes, Red (bell) Pepper and Apple Salad 98
Grapefruit: Orange, Grapefruit and Lime Segments with Mint 15
Guinea Fowl, Roast 139
Guinness: Herbed Beef Guinness Casserole 119

Haddock, Smoked: in quiches 57
  Smoked Haddock Chowder 86
Halibut (bell) Pepper and Mushroom Plaited Pastry Loaf 117
Ham: in baked potatoes 108
  Braised Ham Steak with Pineapple and Herb Topping 29
  Fried Ham and Cheese Sandwich 109
  in profiteroles 55
  in sandwiches 109
  Sweet Roast Ham 89, 90–1
Hazelnuts: Pecan, Pineapple, Ginger and Hazelnut Frangipane 77, 82–3
Herbs: Braised Ham Steak with Pineapple and Herb Topping 29
  Cheese and Herb Balls 40
  Cheese and Herb Pâté 148
  dried 147, 151–2
  herb oils 148
  herb vinegars 147
Herbed Beef Guinness Casserole 119
High teas 84–99
Hollandaise: Smoked Salmon in Walnut Spinach Nest with Poached Egg and Hollandaise 138
Horseradish Cream 25

Iced Tea 66–7, 68, 76–7
Individual Pizzas 49, 50–1, 52–3

Jelly: Simple Wine Jelly 140
  Sweet and Sour Jellies 154
Junket 134–5, 137

Kebabs, vegetable 60–1, 62–3
Keta (red caviar) 13, 17, 57
  New Potatoes with Sour Cream and Keta 20
  Curried Drop Scones with Smoked Trout, Horseradish Cream and Keta 25
Kidneys in Cream with Port Wine and Croûtons 27

Lamb: barbecued 34

157

Lamb (continued)
Lamb Cutlets (rib lamb chops) in Orange and Ginger with Pineapple **120**
Leg of Lamb Studded with Preserved Ginger, Garlic and Rosemary, with Two Sauces 141, 142–3, **144**
Macaroni Lamb Savoury **118**
Picnic Meat Pie **60**
Plaited Pastry Loaf **116**
in profiteroles 55
Savoury Lamb with Coriander (pizza) **53**
Savoury Mince Turnover **49**
Savoury Mince Topped with Baked Potato Circles **26**
Leek: in quiches 57
in vegetable kebabs 60–1
in vegetable casserole 121
Lemon: Lemon Curd 13, 26, 33, 73, 78, 81, 89, 90–1, 146, **154**
Syllabub **139**
Tangy Lemon Cream **122–3**, 124
Lemonade 65, **81**, 82–3
Lentil Soup 104, 105, 106–7
Lime: Apple, Lime, Grape and Mushroom Salad **96**
Lime Jelly **154**
Orange, Grapefruit and Lime Segments with Mint **15**
Loin of Pork Marinated in Coconut Milk with Pineapple, and Coffee Cream Sauce **129**, 130–1
Lunches 32–63, 126–145

Macaroni Beef or Lamb Savoury **118**
Marmalade Popovers 13, **26**, 29, 30–1
Marshmallows: barbecued 34
Home-made 34, **80**
Shortbread, Chocolate, Marshmallow Tartlets **80**, 82–3
Melon with Raspberry Purée **125**
Meringue Basket **132–3**
Mini-Twirl Sandwiches 65, 66–7, **68**
Mini Wheatmeal Loaves 37, 38–9, **69**, 93, 94–5, 100
Mint: Courgettes (zucchini) in Orange Juice Topped with Sour Cream and Mint (salad) **96**
Orange, Grapefruit and Lime Segments with Mint **15**
Pineapple and Mint Sauce **144**
Muesli (granola) 10–11, 12, 13, **14**
Mushrooms: Apple, Lime, Grape and Mushroom Salad **96**
in baked potatoes 108
Chicken, Mushroom and Sweetcorn (corn on the cob) Turnover **49**
Halibut, (bell) Pepper and Mushroom Plaited Pastry Loaf **117**

Mushroom and Walnut Salad **93**, 96
in quiches 57
Savoury Mushroom Caps **35**
Mushroom Pâté 21, **149**

New Potatoes with Sour Cream and Keta 10–11, 13, **20**

Olives: Cheese, Bacon and Olive Pizza **53**
Onion: in baked potatoes 108
Cheese, Chutney and Onion Turnover **49**
Onion and Red (bell) Pepper Marmalade 112, **153**
Pickled Onions **153**
Pork with Sage, Onion and Apple Purée (pizza) **53**
Tuna, Pea and Onion Fish Cake **25**
in Vegetable Kebabs 61
Orange: fresh orange juice 12–13, 14, 81, 96, 113
Lamb Cutlets (rib lamb chops) in Orange and Ginger with Pineapple **120**
Orange Cheese Balls **40**
Orange, Grapefruit and Lime Segments with Mint **15**, 21, 22–3
Orange Wedge Cake 66–7, 68, **76**
in salads 93, 94–5, 99
segmenting 15
Watercress, Orange and Walnut Salad with Bacon Bits **98**

Parsnips: purée 112–13
Passionate Figs with Brandy **14**, 17, 18–19
Passionfruit 14
Pastry: Cheese **141**
Choux **54**
Sweet **78–9**
Wholewheat **56–7**, 85
Pâté, Calvados Apple Duck Liver 114–15, **117**
Peaches, Poached Spiced **125**
Peanut Butter 55, 57, 87, 108
Peas: in baked potatoes 108
Beef Tomatoes Filled with Peas **105**
in quiches 57
Salmon, Egg, Rice and Pea Plaited Pastry Loaf **116**
in soup 105
Tuna, Pea and Onion Fish Cake **25**
Pecan nuts: Pecan, Pineapple, Ginger and Hazelnut Frangipane 77, 82–3
in profiteroles 55
in salad 99
Peppers (bell peppers): in crudités 36

Halibut, Pepper and Mushroom Plaited Pastry Loaf **117**
Onion and Red Pepper Marmalade 112, **153**
in quiches 57
Red Pepper Cream Sauce **144**
Cottage Cheese with Grapes, Red Pepper and Apple Salad **98**
in vegetable kebabs 61
White Fish with Red Pepper, Grated Courgettes (zucchini), and Lime (fish cake) **24**
Pernod: Tomato and Pernod Sorbet **128**
Pickled Onions **153**
Picnics 32–63, 89
Picnic Meat Pie 41, 42–3, **60**
Pig's trotters (feet) 41, 104
Pineapple: Lamb Cutlets (rib lamb chops) in Orange and Ginger with Pineapple **120**
Loin of Pork Marinated in Coconut Milk with Pineapple **129**, 130–1
Pecan, Pineapple, Ginger and Hazelnut Frangipane 77, 82–3
Pineapple and Mint Sauce **144**
in quiches 57
Pizzas, Individual 49, 50–1, **52–3**
Cheese, Bacon and Olives **53**
Pork with Sage, Onion and Apple Purée **53**
Salami and Tomato Provençale **52**
Savoury Lamb with Coriander **53**
Smoked Salmon, Waterchestnut and Fennel **53**
Plaited Pastry Loaf 121, **116–17**, 122–3
Curried Vegetable and Chutney **117**
Halibut, (bell) Pepper and Mushroom **117**
Salmon, Egg, Rice and Peas **116**
Savoury Mince **116**
Poached Spiced Peaches and Apricots **125**, 132
Popovers, Marmalade **26**
Pork: barbecued 34
Loin of Pork Marinated in Coconut Milk with Pineapple **129**, 130–1
Picnic Meat Pie **60**
Pork with Sage, Onion and Apple Purée (pizza) **53**
Porridge, Overnight **16**
Port: in dips 37
Kidneys in Cream with Port Wine and Croûtons **27**
Stilton, Port and Walnut Balls **40**
Potatoes: Baked 100, **108**, 127
Chips (French fries) **88**
in fish cakes 24–5
French Bean and New Potato Salad **97**

Potatoes (continued)
mashed 127
New Potatoes with Sour Cream and Keta **20**
Savoury Beef or Lamb Topped with Baked Potato Circles **26**
Poussin (Rock Cornish hen), Chilled Jellied **41**
Profiteroles **54**, 57, 58–9

Quail, Boned Stuffed ,**44**, 62–3
Quiches 21, 39, **56–7**, 85

Radicchio 37, 38–9, 99
Radishes: in baked potatoes 109
Radish, Apple and Celeriac (celery root) Salad **98**
Raspberry: Melon with Raspberry Purée **125**
Raspberry Purée 61, **124**
Raspberry Syllabub Trifle 41, 42–3, **61**, 84
in tartlets 78–9
Redcurrant Jelly 79, 113, 117, **154**
Rhubarb Cooked in Ginger Beer 10–11, 14, **16**
Rice: Salmon, Egg, Rice and Pea Plaited Pastry Loaf **116**
Roast Beef 134–5, **136**
Roast Guinea Fowl **139**
Rock Cornish Hen: *See* Poussin
Rosemary: Leg of Lamb Studded with Preserved Ginger, Garlic and Rosemary 142–3, **144**
Rutabaga: *See* Swede

Sage: Pork with Sage, Onion and Apple Purée (pizza) **53**
Salads 92–9, 127
Apple, Lime, Grape and Mushroom **96**
Broad Beans with Bacon Bits **97**
Cottage Cheese with Grapes, Red (bell) Pepper and Apple **98**
Courgettes (zucchini) in Orange Juice Topped with Sour Cream and Mint **96**
Egg, Chive and Sour Cream **96**
French Bean and New Potato with Mustard Dressing **97**
Mushroom and Walnut **93**
Radish, Apple and Celeriac (celery root) **98**
Watercress, Orange and Walnut with Bacon Bits **98**
Salami: Salami and Tomato Provençale Pizza **53**
in soup 104
Salmon: in profiteroles 55
Salmon, Egg, Rice and Peas Plaited Pastry Loaf **116**
Salmon, Fennel and Dill Fish Cake **25**
in sandwiches 68
in turnovers 48

Salmon, Smoked: in savoury custards 21
with scrambled eggs 17
Smoked Salmon in Walnut Spinach Nest with Poached Egg and Hollandaise **138**
Smoked Salmon, Waterchestnut and Fennel Pizza **53**
Sandwiches 65, 84, 85
Cold Toasted Sandwiches **87**
Fried Ham and Cheese Sandwich **109**
Mini-Twirl Sandwiches 65, **68**
Teacakes **86**
Sardines; in baked potatoes 108
in sandwiches 68
Sauces: Cheese **112**
Coffee Cream **129**
Pineapple and Mint **144**
Red (bell) Pepper Cream **144**
Redcurrant, Mustard and Orange **113**
Tomato Provençale **52**
Sausagemeat (bulk sauage) 35, 55
Savoury Baked Potatoes **108–9**
Savoury Beef or Lamb Topped with Baked Potato Circles **26**
Savoury Breadcrumbs 24, 37, 45, 113, 121
Savoury Cheese Balls **40**, 41, 42–3
Savoury Chicken Drumsticks in Yoghurt with Cornflakes **45**
Savoury Custards 21
Savoury Mince (ground beef or lamb): **118**
Macaroni Beef or Lamb Savoury **118**
in profiteroles 55
Plaited Pastry Loaf **116**
Savoury Mince Topped with Baked Potato Circles 13, **26**
Turnover 49
Savoury Mushroom Caps **35**
Savoury Vegetable Casserole 99, 117, **121**
Scones: Drop Scones, Curried **25**
Wheatmeal **81**, 106–7
Shortbread: Chocolate Marshmallow Tartlets **80**, 82–3
Shortbread Rounds **79**, 121, 122–3, 124, 133, 134–5, 137, 139
Simple Wine Jelly 139, **140**
Smoked Haddock Chowder 84, **86**, 90, 90–1
Smoked Salmon in Walnut Spinach Nest with Poached Egg and Hollandaise **138**
Smoked Salmon, Waterchestnut and Fennel Pizza **53**
Sorbet: Tomato and Pernod **128**, 130–1
Soups: Beetroot (beet) and Claret Soup with Yoghurt and Toasted Almonds 134–5, **136**

Curried Leftover Vegetable Soups 58–9, **101**
garnishes for 101
Quick Tomato and Basil Soup **35**, 39
Lentil Soup **104**, 106–7
Smoked Haddock Chowder **86**, 90–1
stock for **104–5**
Vegetable Broth **104–5**, 110–11
Spinach: Smoked Salmon in Walnut Spinach Nest with Poached Egg and Hollandaise **138**
Sponges: 33, 61, 70–1, **72–3**, 139
Stilton cheese: in dips 37
Stilton, Port and Walnut Balls **40**
Stock, chicken **104–5**
Suppers 100–125
Swede (rutabaga): in crudités 36
in vegetable casserole 121
in vegetable kebabs 60–1
Sweetcorn (corn on the cob): in baked potatoes 108
Chicken, Mushroom and Sweetcorn Turnover **49**
Crab with Sweetcorn Fish Cake **24**
in quiches 57
Sweet Pastry 56, 77, **78–9**, 80
Sweet Roast Ham **89**, 90–1
Sweet and Sour Jellies **154**
Syllabub 61, **139**

Tangy Lemon Cream with Toasted Flaked Almonds 121, 122–3, **124**
Tarts and tartlets 65, 66–7, 68, **78–9**, 80, 82–3, **141**, 142–3
Teas 12, 65, 100
Iced Tea 66–7, **76–7**
Teacakes 65, 84, **86**
Tomato: in baked potatoes 108
Beef Tomatoes Filled with Peas **105**
in dips 37
Tomato and Basil Soup with Grated Cheese **35**, 39
Tomato Chutney **149**
Tomato and Pernod Sorbet in Lightly Curried Tulip Case **128**, 130–1
Tomato Provençale **52**, 60, 87, 108, 118
Tongue: in sandwiches 68
Tongue and Cherry Turnover **49**
Trout: Baked Trout in Coriander Butter **45**
Trout, smoked: Curried Drop Scones with Smoked Trout, Horseradish Cream and Keta **25**
in savoury custards 21
with scrambled eggs 17
Trifle: 84, 139
Raspberry Syllabub Trifle **61**
Tulip case **128**

Tuna: Tuna and Cheese Pastry
  Tarlets **141**, 142–3
  Tuna, Pea and Onion Fish Cake
    25
  in sandwiches 68
Turnip: in baked potatoes 109
  purée 112–13
  in vegetable casserole 121
  in vegetable kebabs 60–1
Turnovers: 46–7, **48–9**
  Cheese, Chutney and Onion **49**
  Chicken, Mushroom and
    Sweetcorn (corn on the cob) **49**
  Savoury Mince (ground beef or
    lamb) **49**
  Tongue and Cherry **49**

Vegetable: accompaniments 126–7
  Curried Leftover Vegetable
    Soups **101**
  Curried Vegetable and Chutney
    Plaited Pastry Loaf **117**
  leftovers 6, 101, 104–5, 109,
    110–11
  purées **112–13**, 127
  Savoury Vegetable Casserole **121**
  in soups 35, 101, 104–5, 136
  Vegetable Broth **104–5**, 110–11
  Vegetable Kebabs **60–1**, 62–3

Walnuts: Mushroom and Walnut
  Salad **93**
  in salads 94–5
  in sandwiches 87
  in savoury custards 21
  Stilton, Port and Walnut Balls **40**
  Watercress, Orange and Walnut
    Salad with Bacon Bits **98**
Waterchestnuts: Smoked Salmon,
  Waterchestnut and Fennel Pizza
    53
Watercress: in salads 93, 94–5, 99
  Watercress, Orange and Walnut
    Salad with Bacon Bits **98**
Wheatmeal loaves, Mini 38–9, 69,
  94–5

Wheatmeal Pastry Quiches 37,
  38–9, **56–7**
Wheatmeal Scones 65, **81**, 105,
  106–7
Wine Jelly, Simple **140**

Yoghurt; in dips 37
  in marinade 44
  in salads 96
  Savoury Chicken Drumsticks in
    Yoghurt **45**
  in soup 136
Yorkshire Pudding **26**, 137

Zucchini: *See* Courgettes

ACKNOWLEDGEMENTS

The publishers would like to thank the following for their invaluable assistance and cooperation with photography for this book: Margaret Armstrong; The Steamboat Museum, Bowness-on-Windermere; Harrods; Ena Green Antiques, Nina Fuller, Ruth Davis, Mike 'Unusual Collectables', all at Alfies Antique Market, London, and H. R. Owen Ltd for the generous loan of a Range Rover.